SEDUCING THE BOYS CLUB

Nina DiSesa

CHAIRMAN, McCANN ERICKSON NEW YORK

SEDUCING THE BOYS CLUB

UNCENSORED TACTICS FROM A WOMAN AT THE TOP

 BALLANTINE BOOKS | NEW YORK

Published in the United States by Ballantine Books,
an imprint of The Random House Publishing Group,
a division of Random House, Inc., New York.

BALLANTINE and colophon are registered trademarks
of Random House, Inc.

LIBRARY OF CONGRESS CATALOGING-IN-PUBLICATION DATA

DiSesa, Nina.
Seducing the boys club: uncensored tactics from a woman
at the top / Nina DiSesa.
p. cm.
ISBN 978-0-345-49698-0
1. Women executives. 2. Businesswomen. 3. Career
development. 4. Success in business. I. Title.

HD6054.3.D57 2008
658.4'09082—dc22   2007030713

Printed in the United States of America on acid-free paper

www.ballantinebooks.com

9 8 7 6 5 4 3

Book design by Mary A. Wirth

To my beautiful parents, Leonard and Helen DiSesa,
who were always proud of me and would have been absolutely
delighted to see that I had enough concentration
to actually finish writing a book.

CONTENTS

FOREWORD

James Patterson

vividly remember the first time Nina and I met during a lunch in New York City that she describes in this book. She came off as fiercely competitive, although she claims she was just flirting with me. At any rate, I got used to it. I even began to look forward to our times together.

There are a handful of copywriters who worked for me at J. Walter Thompson while I was running the creative show who went on to write books and novels. I'm proud of all of them. Some, like Nina, are advertising people first and authors second. I think she would be pleased about that distinction, and I believe she will be as successful an author as she is a creative director and chairman.

With this book she combines several disciplines for a wise and devilishly amusing take on how to manage men without us resenting it, if we are smart enough to detect we are being "handled." After all, she was manipulating me with her charm during that first lunch, and like all the rest of the men in her life, I didn't care. Women will devour *Seducing the Boys Club,* and it will be the talk of the town, the talk of many towns, actually. But men should read this book, too. Not that they'll have any defense against a woman who can truly seduce boys clubs, but at least they'll have a good laugh. At any rate, I advised Nina to make it a page-turner, and it is.

Finally, I have to add the opinion that this is an extremely powerful and important book. In writing about one woman's unique and effective approach to not only surviving but *beating* the boys clubs that still control much of the business world, Nina DiSesa has brought to life the reality of those insidious institutions. And she does it with a smile.

SCREW THEIR RULES. NOW TRY SOMETHING ELSE.

About halfway through my career I decided that if I was going to make it in the advertising business I had to aim for the top. After fifteen years, I realized that writing ads and winning creative awards was not going to last forever. This was a young person's business, and if I was going to thrive, I would have to become a manager and a leader before I turned forty-five. For a creative person in advertising, surviving and thriving means running the creative department of an agency. What I didn't realize at the outset was that it also meant breaking down the barriers of that impenetrable bastion of male arrogance and supremacy: "the boys club." This is where male values, behavior, and sexual humor prevail, and where few women are allowed at the top. The only reason we even attempt to join these clubs is that they're fast-paced, exciting, and challenging, and if you know how to win, playing with the boys can be a lot of fun.

The male bastion I wanted to join was advertising, and I wanted to join the biggest club I could find. My stepping-stone to that ultimate job happened in 1991, when I was hired as the executive creative director of J. Walter Thompson's Chicago office. For the previous five years I'd been thriving at the quintessential boys club of McCann Erickson, so I embarked on the Chicago job confident in my ability to control men.

I got a confidence adjustment during the first hour of my first day on the job. The entire agency had gathered to meet me, and I gave everyone an impassioned speech about how we were going to change the fortunes of the agency. We were going to work together to succeed, kick ass, and bring back the glory that was once theirs. Blah-blah-blah-*brilliant,* I thought.

When I finished I expected that there wouldn't be a dry eye in the place—hell, I almost choked *myself* up. But when I asked if there were any questions, there was dead silence. No one had a single question for me. Then, breaking the discomfort that disinterest creates, came a male voice from the back of the room.

"What's your sign?"

Looking back, I wish I had just laughed and said something clever and wildly confident, like:

"The sign of the times, baby." Or something inspiring:

"Pisces. What's your sign? Asshole?"

If I had, I would have gotten the immediate respect of the bad-boy contingent that would seem to elude me for the next three years. But I didn't. I was too surprised at the blatant rejection. So instead I said something dorky, like "Very funny."

In Brooklyn, when we couldn't think of a fast retort to an insult, we'd sneer and say something like:

"Oh, that was so funny, I almost forgot to laugh."

(What does that even *mean*?)

But in those first few moments in Chicago, I had committed a cardinal sin: I had taken something for granted. I thought that just because they needed a savior and I was in savior mode, all those damaged Midwesterners would welcome me with open arms. Instead, they were probably thinking about all the different ways they could string up one more smart-alecky New Yorker and hang her out to dry.

Being assumptive was one more mistake I would have to correct in dealing with men. My first mistake was that I believed in fair play. I thought that if I was a good girl, good things would happen to me. (It's a good thing I didn't hold my breath.)

My second mistake was that I didn't appreciate men and thought they were only useful in bed. In business, I saw them as adversaries.

And the most unfortunate of my errors in judgment was that I thought using feminine wiles was cheating, and that to make it in a man's world, I had to play by all their rules and not complain. It never occurred to me until I was in the thick of it that while some rules are sacrosanct and you need to be aware of them in order to win, many others are not. I had to learn to decide which rules needed to be followed and which ones were okay to ignore. Mainly, I learned it was okay to break with as many conventions as possible and that the squeaky wheels who pull a big load deserve all the oil they can get.

Business Is Not a Level Playing Field

No matter how much we hate to hear this, it's still the truth: Men and women are not equal in the business world. You can ignore that basic fact, you can fight it, or you can use whatever you've got to overcome the imbalance. If you're honest with yourself, you'll recognize that we are managed, rewarded, and regarded differently even when we do the exact same job. We are even punished differently when we commit the same transgressions. Men are often treated as "above reproach." Many of them believe that even blatant misconduct on their part will be ignored, forgiven, or even admired. And often they're right. This is *not* true for women, and we can never forget it. There is a double standard. It stinks, but it's there nonetheless.

A case in point happened between a very senior advertising executive and a woman who worked for him. They were brazenly carrying on an affair, even though they were both married with young children.

One day these two were on a flight to make a big presentation to the board of directors of a very critical client. On the plane ride, which lasted only forty-five minutes, they couldn't restrain themselves, and under the flimsy cover of an airline blanket they spent most of the flight necking. Then it became very obvious to everyone around them that the guy was getting a "special service."

The plane landed, and as everyone prepared to disembark, the people who were sitting near the contented couple got a good look at them. It turned out that most of the people watching the thinly blanketed sex were members of that very board of directors. Two hours later, the ad executive and his mistress had to present to all of them amid whispering, smirks, and poorly disguised laughter. It was humiliating, but the man never showed any sign of remorse. Nor did he suffer any real repercussions. The woman, however, was ridiculed unmercifully behind her back and never recovered her loss of dignity from the escapade. Neither one of them were reprimanded at the time, because the man had an important client in his pocket, but when that client left for another position, both the man and the woman were fired. He was fired a few months later. She was fired the next day.

Ladies, accept the fact that there isn't equality in business, especially not in a boys club. This is true even if you're not having blatant sex and you are doing everything right. Men have been and always will be more privileged than we are. Our biggest mistake is that we don't recognize this fact. We are too damn trusting. We believe in the concept of equality, especially when we are young and just starting out in our careers. We believe that if we are smart and work hard, we will be compensated with money and growth opportunities. We trust in fair play and believe that by following the rules, we will reach our goals. We all believe this. I did, too, when I was a young woman, but I was wrong.

One thing that became obvious was that a lot of these "rules" were created by men but meant only for us. Our male counterparts don't follow all the rules. They know that for them, some rules should be respected, but most of them can be bent. Men are the biggest rule-benders on earth; they just do it intelligently and they do it with one another. Never underestimate the brotherhood of men. Boys clubs thrive on that.

I was certain that by the turn of the century (2000, not 2100) women would find their place alongside men and the world would be far less dominated by males. But we all know it's not happening. It's still big news when a woman is made CEO. Only ten Fortune 500 companies had female CEOs when I was writing this book in 2007. It's tough to get to the top, and if a woman reaches that pinnacle in our male-dominated culture, it's a miracle if she stays there.

The question is, why?

Do Men Resent Us Because They Need Us?

Why do boys clubs still exist? And why is it hard for us to succeed in them, much less lead them? I believe that all companies, governments, and households need women in decision-making roles. It's a dangerous situation when all-important conclusions are drawn by one kind of person. Even if that person is the all-knowing, practically perfect, white, middle-class male.

How many wars might have been avoided if there were more female heads of state, whose instincts would lean toward settling disputes with collaboration and negotiation instead of a show of force? How many CEOs might have retained their jobs (and their freedom) if someone with a more nurturing side had whispered in their ears that what they were doing was selfish, hurtful, and possibly even illegal?

There are real reasons we are not given the top jobs in business, aside from our tendency to propagate the race and become stay-at-home moms. Lots of women opt for careers instead of kids, or careers in *addition* to kids. Why don't more of these women get the breaks they need to climb to the top? And once they get there, why don't they stay there?

The problem is that we don't always know how to fit in to a man's work world. Men see us as unfamiliar, foreign beings they don't really understand, and as a result, they don't feel comfortable with us. Our failure to succeed with them is partially our fault. This is good news. Pilot error is something we can control. Although we can't directly change men's behavior, we can change the way *we* behave, and that can alter the way men feel about us. But before you go through all this effort, first decide how you want to live your life and how much you want to play with these boys. You should want it a lot, because it's not going to be easy; they're not going to invite you in, and you may have to batter down the door to get to them.

But I didn't write this book to convince young mothers to abandon their families and take an ax to that Plexiglas ceiling (so much harder to crash through than a glass ceiling), even though if enough of us smash it, we might eliminate ceilings altogether. I wrote it to arm women with the tools and *confidence* to enter the fray and make career decisions for themselves, to take fate into their own hands, and to climb as high as they want to go. This means going right past that middle-management point of "no return on investment"—when women are passed over in favor of non-childbearing men who are seen to offer a greater ROI.

In order to make these decisions for yourself, you have to understand the very people who would hold you back. That would be men. You must learn how they operate in business and how they regard you. It's not always obvious. You have to decide what you can learn from men. Which of their traits should you emulate? What do you have to do in order to win their respect and turn them into supporters?

There are other things to discover as well. How do you "seduce" these boys and help them see you for who you really are? How do you get into their clubs? When is it okay to manipulate them? And when we get to the top of the ladder and they start working for *us,* how do we manage them and earn their loyalty? What is the one thing "the boys" look for when they are deciding whom they will admire, support, and promote?

They look for themselves!

Men feel comfortable with their own kind, and the more someone reminds a man of himself, the more comfortable he is. If we want to win with them, we have to be more like them. We have to recognize their good qualities and the skills that have made them successful—things like being decisive, focused, and willing to take risks while somehow still having fun throughout the process. If you can tap into your "male" side and not lose any of your wonderfully unique "female" skills, you can win at this game. Most men can't, won't, or don't know how to get in touch with their "female" side, and this puts them at a disadvantage.

Still, winning at this game requires work. All the men around you, including those above, below, and right next to you, can make you happy or break your spirit. How can you get these men on your side without compromising your standards or your integrity? After all, you deserve to be working alongside them, and when it's time, you'll deserve to have them working for *you.*

This book is about how a woman like me, who was insecure and unfocused, succeeded in a business environment that has always rewarded its men at the expense of its women. But even more important, it's about how you can learn to do it, too, and do it even better than I did. I had a slow start. Before I could get in touch with my male side I first had to find the *woman* in me who was capable of becoming a chairman and chief creative officer in the quintessential boys club of advertising. That was a huge first step, and I had a steep learning curve.

The biggest lessons I learned along the way were: Always "read" the room (you're less likely to step in shit); don't wallow in decision anxiety (it makes you look weak); and don't confuse seduction with sex (one is a brilliant business tactic; the other isn't).

The most helpful things I discovered were little secrets and insights about understanding and managing men. We have to seduce them without sex and manipulate them without malice. And we must like them. If we play our hand correctly, we can work alongside men as equals, and when the time comes, we can protect them, lead them to greatness, and even make them better men—at least the ones who have room for improvement.

This requires effort and patience, but deep down we are biologically wired to succeed. We have the natural talents for some of it; the rest we can learn.

I can assure you that I wasn't born to play the role of chairman in a boys club—far from it. There was never a silver spoon in my mouth or anywhere near me. I didn't go to an expensive prep school or an Ivy League college. I never learned to play golf (a major male-bonding activity), and although I know the difference between a football, basketball, and baseball (different shapes, right?), I have never been passionate about sports.

But I *did* learn and master the Art of S&M (Seduction and Manipulation). Having done that, I can make it easier for you to do the same. You just have to wrap your head around the fact that hard work and talent isn't going to be enough to propel you to the top. Seduction and *benevolent* manipulation will help turn being a woman into a huge advantage instead of something you need to overcome. It's also the clearest and fastest way to win with men.

All you need to do is break some of those time-honored rules along the way. They weren't working for us anyway.

Screw the rules. Make up your own. Am I repeating myself? Good.

1

EVERYTHING
COUNTS

My own mother-in-law—a dear, sweet lady who usually never had an unkind word about anyone—thought women like me were "buttinskies." This is a term she used for women who insinuated themselves into a man's world. We butt in. This was the attitude of a University of Michigan college graduate who'd had a thirty-five-year career in the medical profession. Even *she* thought women should know their place, and it wasn't at the head of the boardroom in a boys club. Her name was Muriel, and shortly before she died in 2004 at ninety-six, she took my hand and told me she was proud of me. "You're the best buttinsky I've ever known," was the last thing she ever said to me.

My own mother was just the opposite. She died at seventy-eight on December 7, 1986, at 3 P.M.—before I ever became a creative director. But when I was made a vice president at Young & Rubicam, she called everyone she knew and said her daughter was *the* vice president of Y&R Advertising! Like there weren't one hundred others with that title.

I learned a lot from both women, but my powers of seduction and manipulation came from my mother, Helen Pennachio DiSesa. Everyone called her Helen Penny to distinguish her from one of my father's sisters, who was also named Helen.

Helen Penny was a master charmer. For one thing, she always got the best service wherever she went, because she was sincerely interested in other people. And she made everything personal.

"You look tired," she would say to a shoe clerk. "I'll only try on this one pair of shoes."

By the time she learned his name, what his hours were, where he lived, and what he really wanted for a career ("You would be a great actor—I can see it in your eyes"), she was his best friend. He happily brought her twenty pairs of shoes to try on and didn't care when she didn't buy even one pair. He was in love. She was also a genius at getting anything she wanted. When she was in the hospital for the last time after her four-year battle with pancreatic cancer, she charmed her doctor into allowing her a ham-and-cheese sandwich when she was supposed to be on a liquid diet. He even went down to the hospital cafeteria and bought it for her. With mustard.

I learned a lot from this woman and from many others along the way. But mainly I learned from my mistakes. I had a very inauspicious beginning to my long ascent to the top of the ladder, but I always looked on the bright side of life. And I figured if I'd started at the top, I would have had nowhere to go but down.

And speaking of going down . . .

1

My Life Started in an Elevator

wasn't actually born in an elevator. Or conceived in one. (How freaky would *that* be? Can you imagine your parents doing it in an elevator?) My *career* started in an elevator, and that was the beginning of my real life, the one I don't look back on and shudder at. It happened one Saturday morning in May. I was with my first husband, a crabby actor I had married four years earlier because I thought I could cheer him up. We had just left our sixth-floor Manhattan apartment to go grocery shopping and, when the elevator doors closed, my husband announced that he had made a decision. I thought he'd decided what he wanted for dinner.

No. He had come to the conclusion that he didn't love me anymore.

When we reached the fourth floor he said that, upon reflection, he probably never had.

By the time we got to the lobby, he confessed that he was in love with another woman.

His entire revelation took less than sixty seconds. Then we went shopping for food. I bought a nice eye-of-round roast. It was on sale. I even cooked it for the little shit.

A week later he packed up and left, and I sprang into action. I painted the bedroom an insomnia-inducing shade of bubble gum pink because he'd never let me decorate our apartment the way I wanted and I needed to assure myself that I was in control of my life. It made me feel like I was sleeping in a giant lung, but I didn't care. It was *my* lung now and I could do with it what I wanted. Then I stopped eating the junk food that was a substitute for you-know-what and lost thirty-five pounds in six months. (Isn't that *great*?) And I quit my job writing resort ads for the Catskills ("Shecky Greene! Here thru Labor Day!"), because I realized I was not going to have a family anytime soon and I needed to think seriously about a career.

Oh, and during those first six months, when I was losing all that weight, I also wept. (I wonder how much of the thirty-five pounds had been water retention.) I cried all the time. Not because I missed my unfaithful husband, but because I felt abandoned, defeated, and convinced that no one would ever love me or even like me. I had no career, no future, and no one to blame.

I was twenty-eight.

Not a very promising beginning on the road to chairman.

I had two big "aha"s after being dumped on that elevator: First, being with the wrong man is worse than having no man at all, and second, I was totally unprepared for a career because I wasn't good at anything. I had to change that quickly and become skilled at something of value. Luckily, I thought I could write. But I had a long road ahead of me, and I had wasted six precious years on a dead-end relationship. (We dated two years before the wedding. You'd think I would have caught on sooner.)

After I got tired of feeling sorry for myself (right around the time my body went from a size 14 to an 8), I found a job as a copywriter at Howard Marks Advertising in New York. Unlike the job writing resort ads for the Catskills, this one required talent. I had to find some of that and fast.

I was hired as a temporary employee after a thirty-minute interview with Howard Marks himself. He didn't need much more time than that to see that I was wounded, insecure, and needy—the three traits he loved the most in another person. It turned out that Howard collected damaged souls. It provided him with built-in dedication from his employees and, to be fair, he also liked to save lives. He certainly didn't hire me for the brilliance of my Catskills resort ads.

All Howard wanted from me was unconditional loyalty and funny radio commercials for the retail clients he served in his hometown of Cleveland, Ohio. Places like the local Arby's franchise and Cleveland Tux Rentals. I was positive that I could be funny—if I could just stop crying.

Working for Howard was my first experience being in the power of a controlling person. He combined skillful manipulation with a sprinkling of child psychology and a pinch of positive reinforcement. I watched a master control *me* in the same way he controlled all the people who worked for him. I saw him get better work from us all without really asking for it. He did it by making us desperate for his approval and by keeping us off balance. We never knew when the happy, charming Howard would show up for work or when the mean, irritable Mr. Marks would be joining us for a verbal whipping. I think this was more a result of his blood-sugar levels than any psychological issue. He was always on a diet and believed he could eat as much as he wanted if the foods were low in fat. He would eat mounds of steamed shrimp for lunch and point to his overflowing plate and say gleefully, "No calories!" Looking back, I'm sure he had high cholesterol as well as diabetes.

In his more lucid moments, Howard wished for creative nirvana.

"If I could only *convince* people to be more creative," he told me once, "I would be rich."

Howard couldn't enforce creativity, but he could give us enough confidence to open up our minds and release any dormant brilliance lurking inside.

He also taught me that you couldn't legislate loyalty. Howard knew how to make us *want* to please him, especially on the days we were confident he wouldn't fire us all in a fit of fury. Here's how he seduced and manipulated me:

Howard would give me an assignment to write a radio script. I'd write something and drop it in his in-box for approval. Then he would return it with his comments and the reason he rejected it. (There was only one reason: "Not funny!") After a few misses, I finally got a script with "Good." written in the upper-right-hand corner. I was really pleased. When I showed the script to the people on his staff, they kindly explained his code to me. "Good." with a period meant it was just okay and he could live with it. It was up to me to decide whether I could live with it. "Good!" with an exclamation point meant he liked it. After that, they said, his comments were self-explanatory.

The first time I got a "Good!" from Howard I felt great! But I wanted his approval so much that I would try to do even better. When a script finally came back with "GREAT!" written in the upper corner, I was elated. That spurred me on to take bigger chances, and with my confidence growing, I would dash out scripts that actually brought a smile to my own miserable face. After a while, I got the greatest compliment Howard could give: A script came back to me with "BRILLIANT!!!" scribbled at the top.

Yes, I thought, I *was* brilliant. It was a radio spot for Cleveland Tux about a hapless groom who forgot he was getting married until the day before the wedding. His friends urged him to go to Cleveland Tux because he could get fitted quickly, and if his fiancée killed him, he could always use the tux for his funeral. "It's a win-win situation," his best man assured him.

At the end of my thirty-day trial period, Howard put me on staff, and I soaked up everything he had to teach me. Not just his advice about writing humor, which was: "Don't bore me, okay?" but also how he deftly seduced and manipulated his staff so that we behaved the way he wanted us to. At first I thought it was wrong to be so manipulative. The very word conjures up self-serving evil, but I think there are many kinds of manipulation. The most common kind is really very normal: It's an instinct embedded in our DNA. Aren't we born trying to control our universe from our first breath of life? What do you think all that crying is about when we slip out of the womb?

You are probably a master manipulator already and you don't even know it. When you were just days old, you were already controlling your poor mother. You quickly learned that if you wail, your mother springs into action with a whole repertoire of services for your personal pleasure. You cry and she picks you up. Or she feeds you, changes your diaper, or just cuddles with you until you feel better. She's thrilled when you stop crying. It didn't take you long to put this together. What power you had over her.

When you were just eight months old, you lowered your eyes and looked at your father through your lashes. You have already wrapped the guy around your tiny finger, and he will stay there until your hormones kick in at around thirteen and you become a temporary monster.

Then you're a mother yourself and the chickens come home to roost. Your seven-year-old son wants a video iPod. You say he's too young. He says all the other kids in his class have one. You say you don't care. He says he will carry out the garbage every night until he goes to college. You say . . . *And,* he continues, he will never wash his little sister's dolls and dry them in the microwave ever again. He will be nice to her in perpetuity. You ask if he knows what that word means. He says "until the end of time." He looked it up on www.dictionary.com.

You get him the iPod.

The most successful people in business, warfare, politics, and life itself are masters of the art of manipulation. The really good ones, like Howard, are masters of *seduction* and manipulation, or S&M as I like to call it. This combination is a psychological powerhouse, but in order for it to work, the two skills have to be inextricably linked. Manipulation without seduction breeds only contempt and resentment. Seduction without manipulation may be fun for a while, but it doesn't get you anywhere except in trouble. People who use their skills at S&M for their own selfish reasons deserve to be held in contempt. The ones who do it for a higher cause are considered to be great leaders. If the word "manipulation" irks you, substitute "invisible persuasion." Same thing.

After almost two years with Howard, I had written and produced hundreds of radio commercials but only one television commercial. And that experience almost turned me off to advertising before I really even got started.

We were selling a diaper service, and we had cast the most adorable nine-month-old girl as The Baby. The problem was that this baby was too happy. She loved the cameras and the lights, and everything made her giggle and gurgle with delight. I was crazy about this kid, and whenever we had a break, I held her and played with her. But there was one scene where she was supposed to cry because her diaper was wet.

"Let's just wait until she gets tired, then she'll cry, right?" I said to the mother. But the mother just shook her head sadly. This was her very first television commercial, and she didn't know enough to lie.

"She never cries," the mother said in disgust.

"She never cries?" the director, lighting guy, and I asked in unison.

"Never."

The lighting guy started shutting down the lights.

"No, wait," the mother said.

Then she picked up her beautiful baby girl and bit her on the leg.

The baby wailed. The lights went back on. We shot the scene.

Nobody seemed to mind, but I have never forgotten the look of betrayal on that baby's face when her own mother hurt her—for a lousy commercial.

My first reaction was that I needed to get out of this business. But then I talked myself out of it. I liked advertising; I just didn't like that part of it. Maybe if I went to another agency, a bigger shop with a good creative reputation, things like this wouldn't happen. People wouldn't bite little babies to get a scene shot. That wishful thinking, along with the certainty that I would never get ahead in advertising writing radio commercials for retail stores in Cleveland, Ohio, lit a fire under me.

Right around this time, a young, ambitious creative director named Bill Westbrook had been trying to recruit me for his agency in Richmond, Virginia, a prestigious, regional shop called Cargill, Wilson & Acree. I had met Bill while I was being a dutiful wife to my first husband, the dour actor. At the very beginning of our marriage, my husband had been drafted and sent to Fort Jackson in Columbia, South Carolina, and I followed him. There I met Bill at a small agency called Newman, Saylor & Gregory. They needed an assistant art director. I lied about having the skills they needed (making Photostats on a cameralike machine, primarily), and they hired me. I couldn't art direct my way out of a paper sack, and I kept jamming the Photostat machines I was supposed to be an expert at running. I'd never even seen one before. After the third re-

pairman came, I begged him to teach me how to make stats without causing a crisis, and I got pretty good at it. Even so, Bill knew
me for the fraud I was as an art director and kept slipping me ads
to *write*. He always thought I could be good, and when he became
the creative director at Cargill several years later, he tried to hire
me. He tried to hire me for two years.

But leaving New York permanently and moving to the South
was a big step for an unsophisticated Italian American from Brooklyn who had been on an airplane only once. I was scared. Bill was
persistent, though, and I finally consented. I had nothing to lose. I
was thirty years old and desperate, and sometimes desperation can
give even a coward the semblance of a backbone.

Richmond started me on a path toward something I didn't
know existed: that shatterproof Plexiglas ceiling. I didn't have any
long-term ambitions to rise through the ranks. I just wanted to be
good at something that would be valuable to an employer and
would earn me the respect I craved and the money I wanted. But I
had two seminal moments in Richmond that changed my life. The
first one brought home the inequities of being a woman in a man's
world.

I had been working for a year on Ethyl Automotive Additives
(a competing brand with STP Motor Oils). As I learned about its
line of products, I also learned about a car's engine. Soon I could
change spark plugs, and eventually an oil filter. I learned how to
check oil levels, change the rubber on a windshield wiper, and
measure the air pressure in tires. I could even *change* a tire as long
as someone strong would unscrew the lug nuts. Although I had
never actually met the client at Ethyl, he was always telling our account managers how happy he was with his ads and especially the
copy. I was proud of the job I was doing.

One day, while the client was at the agency, an ad needed a
major rewrite, and it had to be done quickly. So I was called in to
the meeting and introduced as the writer who'd been doing his ad-

vertising for the past ten months. He was very polite to me (this should have been my first inkling that something was amiss—I had always heard that he was rowdy and funny with the men), and he explained what had to be done to his ad. I solved the problem in the meeting room while he was watching. I left thinking that if this guy liked me before, now he must *love* me. He *loooves* me. I solved his problem on the spot.

The next day the client asked that I be taken off his business. He said he didn't want a girl writing his ads. I was shocked.

"But I've been writing his freaking ads for ten months. And I solved his freaking problem on the spot. What an asshole!"

Only I didn't say that or anything else. I accepted it, just as I'd accepted hurtful, unfair things all my life. Like with my ex-husband's infidelity and divorce, instead of getting mad at him I got mad at *me*. It's called depression.

Why was my self-esteem so low? I'd had a happy childhood with unconditional parental love and support. My mother and father gave me the confidence to believe that I could be everything I wanted to be. But maybe I didn't want to *be* anything.

It wasn't like that in the beginning of my life. In grade school I was considered a "gifted" child, and they put me in a special class, where half the day was spent in creative pursuits. I painted, made clay models, and sculpted things out of papier-mâché. In the fourth grade I appeared on a local TV show because I had made a six-horse carousel out of ordinary household objects like tampons, empty toilet paper rolls, empty spools of thread (which weren't empty when I found them), and my father's pipe cleaners.

In the sixth grade, though, at just eleven years old, it all turned to shit. Everyone in our school district (and probably all over the country) was made to take tests that measured our IQs. Mine was high enough for me to be placed in a Special Progress program, which combined three years of middle school into two. Staying in this program meant I would graduate from high school just three months after my sixteenth birthday. My family and teachers were so proud of me, but the downside of this achievement was that for the first time in my life, I had serious competition. For the next two years I was locked in a class with thirty-four geniuses. Suddenly, I went from being a gifted child to the weakest link. I knew I wasn't a genius and was convinced that the test results were wrong. Someone had made a terrible mistake. I didn't belong in the Special Progress program. I was a fraud. Soon I started having a recurring nightmare, which lasted for the entire two years of the program. Someone would walk into the class and call out my name:

"NINAAAAAA DEEESAAAAYZAAAAAAA."

"What?"

"COME WITH ME."

"Why?"

"THERE'S BEEN A TERRIBLE MISTAKE."

"Oh God."

And I get hauled out of the class amid the murmurings of my classmates, who knew all along that I was a fraud.

"I *knew* it," some kids whispered loudly.

"It was obvious she didn't belong here with *us*."

"She didn't know *any* answers."

Thus, my long road to insecurity started when I was twelve years old and lasted until the end of my thirtieth year, when I metamorphosed almost overnight from a shy and insecure loser to a first-rate conceited jerk.

And that was my second epiphany. If you want to become a jerk, life will offer you ample opportunities to achieve your goal.

Here's the pit I fell into and never saw coming:

Since my advertising career started late in my life, it was easy for me to become obsessed with catching up, and in Richmond, I worked all the time. By the end of my first year I'd written and produced hundreds of newspaper and magazine ads. Up until this point in my life, my insecurity made me very accommodating in that I rarely fought for my work—or anything else for that matter. If someone thought an ad wasn't good enough, I would keep working at it or try a different approach. I was probably *too* accommodating, too eager to please, too *nice*. That didn't last.

At the end of that first year, the agency entered almost all of our work in the regional division of a prestigious national creative show. The night of the awards ceremony came and, although I didn't want to go, I was pressured into attending with the rest of the agency. The auditorium where the awards were being presented was packed with everyone who worked in advertising in Richmond. I was so intimidated, I sat in the very rear of the huge room and hoped no one would notice me.

Then, in the very first category, one of my ads won first place. I had to stand up and walk from the back of the room to the front, where someone handed me my award, shook my hand, and posed with me for a photo. Then I walked back to my seat. I did this all alone, because my art director/partner was a recluse and didn't feel compelled to show up that night.

Almost as soon as I sat down, another of our ads won first place in another category. Then another. Every time they called out my name, I had to walk the entire length of the room to get to the stage and accept the award. After it happened three or four times, the photographer stopped taking my picture. I considered sitting closer to the stage, but I worried that it would look presumptuous on my part, as if I *expected* to keep winning. So I trudged back to my seat in the last row until they called my name again and again and again. After several more trips, the audience got tired of applauding for me. Eventually, they started laughing when my name was called. Toward the end I thought I detected more than a few groans. My ads won twenty-seven awards that night, and everyone in the Richmond ad community learned my name and what I looked like. From the front and the back.

Once I became famous in Richmond, I became a nervous wreck. Soon after, I became a jerk. I was still a basically nice person, but with a decidedly hysterical bent. As time wore on, I became increasingly fearful that my newly won creative reputation was a fluke and that one bad ad could send me back to oblivion.

"NINAAAAAA DEEESAAAAYZAAAAAAA. GIVE BACK YOUR TWENTY-SEVEN AWARDS."

It made me wary of anyone who tried to tamper with one of my ads. And I was *loudly* wary. Unfortunately, any kind of venting is normal on the creative side of the advertising business, and no one feels the need to keep the creative people in check. I think it is commonly believed that if we are restrained in any way, it will somehow affect the chaotic freedom that fuels our creativity.

Can I just say that this is crap?

We are just being rude, and the more we get away with it, the more insufferable we become. The big question is, Why are we so volatile? The answer: We are scared shitless. All of the time.

All creative people who make a living by their wits can become crazy at one time or another: writers, painters, musicians, actors, directors. We are, on and off, certifiably nuts. It's why we do things like drink or use drugs excessively, have promiscuous sex, and lose our temper and throw phones at people. All of us in creative fields are always afraid, because we believe talent is arbitrary and creativity is subjective.

We hate subjectivity.

A creative idea that we think is brilliant could, in fact, just be a pile of crap, and there are always lots of people who might notice this and be inconsiderate enough to bring it to our attention. It makes us insecure.

We hate insecurity, too.

The only thing we hate more than our own pathetic lack of confidence is Public Humiliation, and we will lash out at anyone who forces us into that horrible space.

This is what happened to me. I didn't drink, do drugs, or have promiscuous sex (who had time?), but I did lose my temper. Once it almost killed me.

The first total meltdown I ever had was shortly after that award-winning night in Richmond. I was sitting in my office eating a Granny Smith apple when one of the agency's account managers, a quiet ex–Army officer named John, came in with a print ad that I'd written for Planters National Bank. The client had changed my headline, and John had allowed it. (At Cargill, this was taboo. No one but the writer could change copy.)

The full-page newspaper ad that caused the trouble was for a promotion to attract new savings customers. In order to lure people to the bank, it offered place settings and serving dishes every time someone made a deposit in a passport savings account. It was back during the "free toaster" era of banking. Remember those days? When bankers actually competed for your business with bribes? No? You're lucky. It means you're young.

My headline was:

If you can't save for love or money,
how about for a few free dishes?

The client thought it was too flippant and didn't sell hard enough. He wanted the headline to read:

If you won't save for our 5% passbook interest rate,
how about for a lovely 5-piece place setting?

I should have calmly said, "Well, John, *that's* lame." Or something even stronger such as, "I am *not* changing this headline. John."

If I had known then what I learned much later in my career, I would have been diplomatic and manipulated John with seduction and charm. I would have smiled sincerely at this account manager who was ruining my reputation and said, "Well, John, that's certainly more to the point. You and the client are very *clever* to 'cut to the chase,' as it were . . . *however* . . . it does *lack* the element of surprise, doesn't it? It doesn't impart a *human* personality for the bank, like the original headline did. Plus, and I say this with all due respect, it's a little . . . flat, wouldn't you say? *JOHN?* I mean, John." Smile. Flutter eyelashes. "Really. Why change something so perfect?"

But instead what came out of my mouth was:

"Oh, *God.* Are you *SHITTING* me? That totally *SUCKS!* It *FUCKING RUINS* the whole *FUCKING AD. AUUUUGGGGGGHH-HHHHH."*

Believe it or not, I had never used the verb "to fuck" in any context until I was thirty years old. But by the time I was thirty-one, I was using it as a verb, adjective, adverb, noun, and—in moments of sheer frustration—as a hyphen, as in un-*fucking*-acceptable.

At Cargill, I used the word all the time. Unfortunately, as I was using it this time, I was also screaming at poor John with my mouth full of a Granny Smith apple. I started to choke, but I couldn't stop screaming at him. Now apple pulp is spewing all over him and my desk. I'm turning blue (as he told me later), so he smacks me hard on the back and a chunk of apple flies out of my mouth and lands on the typed copy of the client-butchered ad that he'd placed on my desk. *SPLAT.*

"You shouldn't scream with your mouth full," John says, and then calmly walks out of my office jingling the loose change in his pocket. He always did that and it drove me crazy, but his jingling also signaled when he was coming down the hall to my office, and I could usually duck into the bathroom before he reached me.

I scraped the apple off my copy and changed the headline back to what I'd written. Eventually, we reached a compromise and ran the ad with this headline:

If you won't save for our 5% interest rate,
how about for a few free dishes?

It was better the original way. The unexpected, flip attitude would have made the ad stand out more and grab the reader's attention. And it was certainly more human. But I was ahead of my time. Banks didn't *want* to be human back then. They wanted to earn your trust with free small household appliances.

So what can you learn from this? Clearly, one lesson is not to have meltdowns while you're eating, but what else? I didn't win my battle. They still changed my headline. And I didn't walk away from that incident with a higher standing in the agency. Taking a stand that way made some people afraid of me, but it didn't garner me any more respect from the account managers. The creative people thought it was funny, and I got some of their misguided admiration, but the rest of the agency thought I was just a hothead from New York and too big for my britches. It took a long time to live that down. Was it worth it? Maybe, if I had saved my headline. But I didn't even do that.

For the most part, my time in Richmond set the tone for the next two decades of my career. I did a lot of things differently on my way up the ladder in the advertising business. I wasn't a shrinking violet with the men I worked with, and I didn't mind having meltdowns in front of them. That scared them sometimes, but since they were meltdowns (things you do by yourself) as opposed to fights (things you do with them), they learned not to take my fits personally. The meltdowns revealed my vulnerability to my male colleagues, and at times I even broke Cardinal Rule #1 by crying in front of them. None of this hurt me in my journey up the ladder.

I had a late start on my path, but being older gave me maturity and insights about people I didn't have when I was fresh out of college. I knew, for instance, that to control my destiny, I had to win over the people who could help me and diffuse the people who were out to hurt me. I had to learn how to seduce and manipulate everyone, not just men, and I had to do it in a way that made people love me, not resent me.

The only way I knew how to accomplish this was by putting other people's interests first, because that's all anyone really cares about. "What's in it for me?" It's the most powerful question in the advertising business and in life itself. Even the most philanthropic people are generous because it makes *them* feel good.

I also tried to help everyone I seduced and manipulated to be better people, not just better at their chosen professions. I'm no Mother Teresa, believe me; I did this mainly because I found it was easier to win people over when I acted unselfishly.

There are a lot of labels for my process, but it is really a combination of seduction and manipulation, as odious as that "M" word is to some people. But the people I worked with insist that I "maneuvered" people and events, not manipulated them. Call it what you will, it has been my style from almost the beginning and one of the reasons (I believe) for my success.

I learned it from advertising. I learned a lot from the ad biz.

2

Hearts Trump Heads

If people responded to pure logic, there would be no need for the kind of emotional advertising we do today. We'd have solid, clear-cut reasons for why one brand, product, service, political candidate, or conviction should be preferred over another. We wouldn't ask people to feel something for a brand. We certainly wouldn't need creative people racking their brains trying to think of clever ways to make you fall in love. That's really what advertising people do, in a nutshell. We use charm, humor, surprise, intrigue, special effects, celebrities, kids, and dogs in our attempt to make the consumer fall in love with a brand or a cause or our next president. We're going for love, because we know, without a shadow of a doubt, that in the battle between the head and the heart, *the heart always wins.*

If the head won, all ads would say the same thing:

Two Good Reasons to Drink Coca-Cola Instead of Pepsi
Four Really Good Reasons to Use MasterCard Instead of Visa
Six Most Excellent Reasons to Use Verizon Instead of AT&T

You probably can't wait to hear what those *most excellent* reasons are.

If logic were all you needed as a parent, it would be easier to raise children:

Seven Important Reasons You Should Put Your Toys in the Toy Box When You're Finished Playing with Them

And think about how easy it would be to stay married:

A Perfectly Reasonable Rationale for Not Cheating On Me

In advertising, we have to make people *want* to prefer Coke instead of Pepsi. We have to make them love the brand and see it as their own. While it may be true that people prefer the taste of either Coke or Pepsi, they are going to start out in life being either Coke people or Pepsi people because of how they feel about the *brand.*

MasterCard and Visa are identical credit cards *by law.* There is no difference between them. And yet, ten years ago, people ignored the MasterCard that was tucked away in their wallet. They used Visa, the card for rich people who were always on skiing vacations in the Alps. That's who they wanted to be. Then McCann did our world-famous "Priceless" campaign that positioned MasterCard users as noble spenders who use credit for the greater good of their relationships, their family, and mankind in general. Today, MasterCard has enjoyed thirteen consecutive quarters of double-digit growth because the brand proved it had a heart and soul. As human beings, we respond to that in a big way. We fell in love with MasterCard. Now the MasterCard brand character is who everyone wants to be.

It's no different in the real world. No four-year-old is going to put his toys away unless you give him a reason to *want* to put them away. And the way to keep a man exclusively in your bed is not with words alone, is it?

All this is done with invisible persuasion. Sometimes this is called motivation, but it's really a form of gentle or benevolent manipulation. We are changing someone's behavior without them realizing it—or resenting it. This skill is appropriate for other industries in the corporate world as well, whether you are selling investments, real estate, or yourself within a company. Invisible persuasion with an emotional payoff is always more potent than logic alone.

Although this works with everyone, it is especially rewarding with men. All of the men in our lives—the ones we work with or live with, admire or desire, and even love or hate—are easier to control if we master the Art of S&M. Men are not that complicated, and I say that with immense respect and affection. I adore men. I admire the way they think—it's different from the way we do, but fascinating nonetheless. I marvel at their sense of humor, their courage under fire, and their ability to compartmentalize— even when that means they are shoving me into a little drawer. I love the way men look and even *walk*. But they're not that hard to seduce and manipulate. First of all, they love seduction, and second, they are oblivious to manipulation. When I suggest this to them, they agree wholeheartedly about the seduction part, but they won't admit that they can be manipulated.

Just be sincere about the seduction, and when you do manipulate them, it has to be for their own good as well. You also have to like them. Most men, who are dense about anything intuitive and have as much sensitivity as a bag of marbles, will notice if you don't like them. *That* they will recognize. And then they will not like *you*.

Embroider this on a pillow, or even better, tattoo it on your wrist:

MEN LIKE WOMEN WHO LIKE THEM.

I suspected this from an early age, but I didn't really put it to the test until I met a man who could bring any sane woman to her knees. As twisted fate would have it, this person, the most frustrating man I ever met in business, was also the one who would become most dear to me. It took about three months for me to go from wanting to kill him (seriously) to protecting him at all costs. Back then we called him Frank "The Madman" Costantini. Once I was able to control him, I knew there wasn't another person *alive* who would ever vex me again. And this held true for almost ten years, until I met a genius named Peter Kim, who vexed me even more. But that story comes much later.

I met Frank at Young & Rubicam in 1985. Back then, he was thought to be a crazy creative person, but he was (and still is) a brilliant conceptual thinker. He looked great, too—very fit, because he was a breathtaking, hotdog skier. And he was a ladies' man. Frank loved gorgeous women, and it didn't matter if they weren't too bright. Women were attracted to him because he was buff and wiry. There wasn't an ounce of fat on his entire body. And although his hair was just starting to thin (much to his horror), he was a handsome devil with a ready grin that melted hearts. I thought this about him even when I fantasized that he would ski off a Double Black Diamond trail in Aspen—his favorite place on earth—and disappear for good.

I don't know if our group creative director made us a team because he was a brilliant judge of character or if he did it because Frank and I were both Italian American. Later on, someone told me that Frank went through his writer partners like popcorn at a double feature, and I turned out to be the only one who could deal with him. (And even I almost didn't make it.) After our partnership produced better work than anyone had expected, I was told that we were perfect together, because Frank had wild ideas and I helped turn them into "solid" advertising. Not exactly a huge compliment to me, but I *was* the more responsible member of the team. He was the hotdogger.

Frank was also a member of an elite posse of egotistical creative people at Y&R (all young men) that thought everyone else at the agency was a hack. In fact, there couldn't have been two more dissimilar people than Frank and me in the history of advertising:

He was hip; I was not.

He was a loose cannon; I was wrapped as tight as a drum.

It was obvious that Frank liked to have fun; I preferred to worry.

He was a shameless womanizer who thought Spandex was a natural fabric, like cotton; I despised and distrusted Spandex.

He already had a stellar creative reputation at Y&R; I was still trying to prove myself as a creative force.

The most challenging difference was that I was a well-rounded creative person with a healthy right brain (creativity, intuition) and a fully functioning left brain (champion of logical thinking and adult behavior). Frank's left hemisphere had atrophied. He was left-brain-dead.

But the biggest disparity between us was age: While he looked ten years older than me, I was actually ten years his senior. (At least I was back then. I believe now we are the same age!)

Yet, in spite of these monumental differences, Frank's only reservation about me was that he assumed I couldn't be funny, and he liked to make funny commercials. I don't know why he thought that about me, but it may have had something to do with the fact that I was always fretting about something and had a permanent scowl on my face. Later, when we started selling our work and shooting TV spots in L.A., we would receive candid photos that were taken on the sets. Frank was always captured grinning and flitting around with the script girls or the makeup artists while I would be sitting by myself, frowning. That was our partnership in a nutshell.

As it turned out, I was a lot funnier than Frank anticipated. Once we stopped fighting, we wrote very amusing spots together and we were always our best audience—we cracked each other up. But anyone who knew us from the start would have bet that we'd be more likely to kill each other. Our first few months were awful. All we did was fight, and we didn't accomplish anything.

Our trouble revolved around the way we worked as a team. We would think of ideas and scenarios together, and if the idea required dialogue, we would split up. I'd go back to my office (or my apartment if it was late at night) and write some scripts. Then I'd return to *his* office (big mistake) and read him the scripts. If he didn't like something, he would say, "*That* sucks." Or: "You call that funny?" I didn't mind those comments, actually. If something wasn't working, it was better to hear it from him, and I trusted his judgment.

It was when he would throw a script back at me and say, "How can you bring me crap like this?" that I would explode. The problem with these fights was that no one could hear Frank's part of the argument. All they heard were my screams. So it would go something like this:

"How can you bring me crap like this?"
"Bring you crap? Bring YOU crap? Who the fuck do you think you are, you little shit?"
"How long did it take to write this? Five seconds? I can't accept this."
"ACCEPT? ACCEPT? Who died and made YOU the freaking King of Comedy?"

And then the final insult:

"Come back when you have something better."
"ASSHOLE, ASSHOLE, ASSHOLE, ASSHOLE!!!"

Word spread quickly that I was difficult, too emotional, and—worst of all—that I was mean to Frank. The members of his posse started to bad-mouth me and, in no time at all, I got the distinct honor of being hated by the creative elite in the agency. Not an ideal situation when my goal was to earn a good creative reputation. I wanted to kill Frank.

Then something happened that opened my eyes.

As it became common knowledge that Frank and I didn't get along, his enemies started crawling out of the woodwork. There were other writers whom Frank had insulted and refused to work with, and these people (all hacks in my opinion) thought they had a kindred soul in me. Was I one of those writers who didn't measure up to Frank's standards?

At first I would defend Frank to these losers.

"He's very bright," I would say. "Bright people like him don't have much patience." I meant to add "with hacks like you," but I restrained myself. After one of his critics approached me for the third time, however, I lost it:

"And what have you done that's so great? Maybe you just weren't good enough to be his partner. Maybe you just *suck*. Ever think of that?"

This didn't do much to help my reputation as a hothead, but at least people stopped talking badly about my Frank.

My Frank?

When did that maniac become *my Frank*? Maybe it was right about the time it became clear that I not only had to protect him, I had to win him over. More important, I *wanted* to win him over. It was essential to earn his respect and have him value me as a true partner. And this had to be done quickly, or we would be separated as a team. If that happened, I knew my next partner would be a loser, someone who wasn't as creative or driven to work as hard as Frank was. That was the one thing I really liked about him. He was as obsessive about the work as I was, and there weren't too many other people like that at Y&R back then. I needed to keep him, and in order to do that, I had to make Frank need me.

My big opportunity came when we got assigned as the backup

team for Frito-Lay's Cheetos brand Cheese Flavored Snacks. Legally, we always had to refer to the product this way the first time it was mentioned in a commercial: Cheetos *BRAND* Cheese Flavored Snacks. We had to say this mouthful in order to protect the trademark, even when it was a line of dialogue coming out of an actor's mouth. For instance, no one in a commercial could say, "Hey, Agatha, want some Cheetos?" We had to say, "Hey, Agatha, want some Cheetos *brand* Cheese Flavored Snacks?"

We fought it like crazy but always lost to the lawyers.

"If we don't protect the trademark, then everyone who makes puffy, corn-based, salty snacks can call their product Cheetos," they would tell us over and over. "Look what happened to Xerox. And Kleenex."

Whatever.

The consumer insight was that these orange, crunchy, puffy, corn-based, salty snacks were so involving and comforting that heavy users said they actually felt better when they had their nose buried in a bag of Cheetos . . . *brand Cheese Flavored Snacks*. They could, literally, block the world out. So Frank came up with this great end line (also called a "slogan").

Eat Cheetos and fuhgedaboudit.

We were madly in love with that line and we created really funny New York–influenced spots that probably would not have appealed to the Bible Belt, but what did we care? "Eat Cheetos and fuhgedaboudit." It was brilliant, and Frank loved to say that line at the end of our TV scripts:

Cheetos brand Cheese Flavored Snacks
Eat Cheetos and fuhgedaboudit.

But it was to no avail. We couldn't sell the line or the campaign. We had to go back to the drawing board. (Now, of course, we say "back to our Macs.")

For our second attempt, we decided to break with our own tradition and actually *look* at the brief we'd been given for the assignment. That meant we had to read the creative strategy prepared by the strategic planners. And guess what? It was *good*! It was all about emotional involvement and the *great satisfaction* that people get when they eat Cheetos. People love their Cheetos. So we connected the dots and assumed that this heavy emotional involvement and satisfaction made the consumer feel happy. I wrote the line:

If you want to be happy, eat more *Cheetos*.

The lawyers got hold of this and tried to make us say:

If you want to be happy,
eat more *Cheetos brand Cheese Flavored Snacks*.

But then they agreed that if we said "Cheetos brand Cheese Flavored Snacks" the first time we mentioned the product, we wouldn't have to say it in the slogan.

We loved the new line. It was not only dead-on the strategy, it actually encouraged consumption. "Eat *more* Cheetos." The campaign was all about people who were made happier because they were eating the salty snack. All the scripts were very funny, and every time I read them people would laugh. Sometimes I would ask Frank if he wanted to read a script or two, but he always declined, so I acted them out. At first I had to perform the spots, because Frank couldn't be bothered with drawing storyboards.* Actually, it *was* more fun to bring the commercial to life instead of holding up a storyboard and stating the obvious:

"In this frame, we have a close-up shot of the Cheetos package."

---

* When we present a TV commercial, we create a storyboard on which we draw enough scenes from the commercial to give people an idea of what the commercial will look like. Then the copy is written next to each scene—or frame—and we present from that. It is also not uncommon for us to just act out the TV spot, but we always have a storyboard that conveys our vision for the spot and for where the products will come in.

It took me a while to realize that Frank had stage fright. If he had to present creative or even just do the setup, he would freeze. But the campaign was getting a lot of attention internally, and I knew he was feeling left out. So I would do the setup (explain the idea of the campaign and how it was on-strategy) and then present one spot. If I got laughs, he would present the second spot. Before long, we were dividing up the scripts between the two of us.

We presented that damn campaign so many times that it soon became "famous advertising" within the halls of Y&R—and it hadn't even gone into production. John Ferrell, our executive creative director, was so in love with the campaign and with us that he made us present it whenever he was in a meeting. It didn't even matter what the meeting was about. He would call us in to his conference room and say, "Do the Cheetos campaign." And we would perform like we were his two dutiful children. We didn't care. We loved presenting the campaign because we always got spontaneous laughter from everyone, and it reinforced our conviction that we were comedic geniuses.

That was the first time that Frank was able to present work without choking up, and over time, the more he presented, the more relaxed he would be and the more confident he would become. In order to help him even more, I wrote one celebrity spot just as a presentation piece, something for him to perform, because it was fun and the kind of spot he could act out really well. We didn't have money in the budget for a celebrity, but everyone loved the script so much, we wound up shooting it anyway. The celebrity was Lee Van Cleef, that wonderful character actor from the spaghetti western genre. He always played the mean bad guy with a scowl on his face. Here was his Cheetos commercial:

CHEETOS "SALOON/VAN CLEEF" TV SCRIPT — :30

Lee Van Cleef bursts into a saloon in the old West. Everyone cowers. He walks menacingly up to the bar, where the bartender has ducked under the counter. When the bartender stands back up, we see that he has grabbed a bag of Cheetos, even though he is quaking in his boots. He clearly needs to be happy about something. While the announcer voice-over suggests that the indulgent taste and crunchy texture of Cheetos (brand Cheese Flavored Snacks) can't help but make you happy, the bartender tries to offer Mr. Van Cleef his bag of Cheetos. Lee smacks the bag away.

"I don't *want* to be happy," he snarls.

(At this point, Frank would give his best imitation of a Lee Van Cleef snarl.)

"Do you think I'd be where I am today if I knew how to *smile*?"

Then we would cut to the product shot with the end line "If you want to be happy, eat *more* Cheetos." And bullets would come blazing into the frame and shatter the type.

Presenting this spot was always Frank's finest moment, and with his new success as a standup comedian came a newfound respect and affection for me. To this day, when he calls me at work he identifies himself as my brother.

The upshot is that Lee Van Cleef went over so well, we shot another celebrity spot with Tom Smothers, then another with a third celebrity. We spent a lot of time in la-la land, second only to Aspen as Frank's favorite place on earth. I hated L.A. I didn't look good in pastels. And there were those blond, Viking-like starlets to contend with, too. Not good.

After our Cheetos triumph, Frank and I were as thick as thieves. A year into our unexpected friendship, we found ourselves dumped by our respective lovers at the same time, and we would come to work every morning crying about how worthless love was as a concept, and then write funny commercials for Cheetos or whatever assignment they threw our way. As long as I had him by my side, I knew we couldn't fail at anything. Plus, he was a lot of fun. We would laugh our heads off all day, and then, when it was time to go home, we would cry about how lonely an empty apartment was. It never occurred to us to go home together. We didn't have that kind of relationship. But it was a great two years for both of us.

Frank taught me that it was a lot easier to win a man over once I stopped resenting him. In fact, it's impossible to seduce and manipulate someone you don't like. Remember that tattoo on your wrist ("Men like women who like them"). Once I started to like Frank, it became easier to ignore his irritating idiosyncrasies, like how he would stare at himself in the mirror behind my desk while I was talking to him. In time, I even found these habits endearing.

I hadn't set out to seduce and manipulate him. Initially, my decision to try to make him look good was a result of my growing affection for him, but it was a mind-opening experience for me. Everyone wants to be a hero, everyone wants to be admired and respected. If you can help someone achieve that status, how can they not like you? Even more important, how can they not *need* you?

I did other things with Frank that became the cornerstone techniques I would use to manage men. For example, if he needed to lean on me, it was always in private. It was never apparent to anyone that Frank had stage fright because I would loosen up our audience before giving him the spotlight. And I protected him. Once I stopped yelling at him, no one else was allowed to abuse him, either outright or by innuendo. It was also important to reinforce his hunk status, assuring him that the small bald spot at the top of his head was hardly noticeable and that he hadn't "lost it" when a woman would break up with him or refuse to date him (a rare event). He needed to know that he had my love unconditionally; it was the only way he could ever trust me with his fragile ego.

Although most of what I did for Frank came from sincerity, my two years with him gave me insights into dealing with difficult and hard-to-control personalities. Manipulating people like this with a deft hand was a way to change behavior without incurring wrath or resentment. It *was* invisible persuasion.

Soon I became very adept at it. It allowed me to maneuver a situation so that the outcome would benefit everyone. But to be honest, all I was really doing was using Howard Marks's old ploy of seduction and manipulation. By the time I became a creative director, I had it down to a science and had mastered several versions:

Seduction and Manipulation with Credible Compliments: Let's say I want my creative people to work harder on an assignment and come up with more than one good idea. (Normally we keep working until we think we have an award-winning, big idea and then we quit.) If I tell them their one idea isn't good enough, I have assaulted their creative egos. And if the team includes a man, I have also somehow maligned his masculinity. I have to get them pumped up to do additional good work. First I want to make them laugh, so I give myself credit for their one good idea—for the sake of credibility.

"Do you see what a brilliant decision I made to put you on this assignment? Is this great creative leadership on my part or what?"

Then I give them credit for whatever they have done so far.

"I knew you would nail this assignment. This is a great idea."

Then I ask for more.

"Can you possibly do it just one more time? No one else is coming up with anything nearly as good as your idea, and I can't go in with just one home run."

They come back with more good work and are now confident that *they are heroes.*

Seduction and Manipulation with Dire Consequences: One of my senior men is behaving very badly. He is treating someone I need and respect shabbily. If I just tell him to stop it, he won't listen to me. If I threaten him, he won't hear me. I have to use a combination of guilt, threats, and hyperbole in order to make him aware of the dire consequences of his actions.

"If you continue to be cruel to Mary, she will quit and it will take me months to find anyone nearly as good as she is. And during those months without her, the entire creative department will go to hell in a handbasket . . . a handbasket. Raises will be delayed, promotions won't go through, and expense checks will be late. No doubt about it. All the people in the creative department will know that you are the cause of their misery and frustration, and you know how ugly that can get. Their lives will be ruined. But even more important, my *life will be ruined. And if my life is ruined, I promise you,* I promise you, *I will make your life* One. Living. Hell."

He sends Mary flowers.

Seduction and Manipulation with Tough but Unconditional Love:
This works with all men when I want them to stop behaving badly.

"I don't know why I'm so crazy about you when you act like such a prick."

What this says is that I love them in spite of their faults, but I still *see* their faults and I want them *fixed.*

All I am trying to do is change the behavior of people who don't necessarily understand that their behavior needs changing. This is very similar to the way we try to change the consumer's behavior with advertising. She isn't buying our mouthwash. We want her to. We can't come right out and ask her to buy our mouthwash; she'll say no. We have to make it seem like it's a good idea. Like it's *her* good idea.

We need a stimulus to get her to respond in our favor.

It's hard to think of a good stimulus that works. That's why we get paid so much money in advertising, but this is also the secret to all behavior.

Stimulus/Response: The Key to Invisible Persuasion

The most effective way to change behavior is to encourage people to arrive at their own conclusions. In advertising, we accomplish this with a behavioral technique called Stimulus/Response, i.e., creating the right stimulus to get the desired response. Here are two famous examples:

Nike didn't want to be just another athletic-shoe manufacturer. When co-founder Philip Knight was CEO, he wanted the brand to have a stronger, more emotional positioning. With the unspoken line of "*Just do it*" and consistently brilliant advertising over the years, Nike carved out its irrefutable global brand equity: "Passion for Sports." They could have easily used a more blatant positioning line, like "We Love Sports" or "Sports Are Our Passion" or even "Sports R Us." But the less obvious "Just do it" was brilliantly passionate. It let the consumer arrive at his or her own conclusion.

The marketers at Verizon Wireless had to convince mobile phone customers that its wireless network was more reliable than any other. They could have given us stats and comparisons until everyone was blue in the face. Instead, they ran a campaign that had the perfect stimulus: an unassuming yet single-minded "Verizon Guy" traveled all over the country doing quality control by asking one simple question over and over again—"Can you hear me now? Good!" The brilliance of this idea was that it used the exact sentence people were already saying into their mobile devices when people *couldn't* hear them.

I was formally introduced to the concept of Stimulus/Response when I worked at J. Walter Thompson. Up until that time, I had been using the psychological behavioral technique instinctively, as most people do. But at JWT it was quantified, and that helped me become much better at creating ads and controlling people and situations.

There are two examples of the relationship between stimulus

and response that we used at JWT, and they serve as a good example of how the mind can be subconsciously manipulated.

The Lesson of Two Signs: You see two signs on the road. Both are selling fresh farm eggs. One sign has a sloppy, hand-painted message with paint dribbling down from the letters. It's written on a large piece of cardboard, and it's leaning against the trunk of a tree:

Farm-fresh eggs —)2 for $)

On the opposite side of the road is another sign—it has the same message, only this sign has been painted professionally. It's crisp and clean, and it's mounted in a large frame that's attached to a metal post:

FARM-FRESH EGGS — $1 PER DOZEN

Which message has affected your behavior? Where do you feel you will get the freshest eggs? You buy the eggs from the farmer who painted his own sign and keep traveling down the road. You see two more signs, this time for flying lessons. One is a rough, hand-painted sign with paint dribbling down from the letters. It's written on a large piece of cardboard that's leaning against a tree:

Professional flying lessons, next right turn.

On the opposite side of the road is another sign. It's printed professionally, looks clean and crisp, and is mounted in a large frame that's attached to a metal post:

PROFESSIONAL FLYING LESSONS, 1 PLAZA NORTH

---

* The signs depicting Stimulus/Response were created by Ralph Rydholm.

These are two classic and very simple examples of Stimulus/Response. You don't want your eggs from a slick operation; you prefer them from the farmer, because he gave you a *stimulus* that said "fresh." He influenced your decision to buy *his* fresh eggs.

Likewise, you don't want to take flying lessons from some fly-by-night person whose idea for giving lessons has just occurred to him. You want a professional instructor who has been doing it for a while—at least, long enough to have a professional sign constructed. That sign made you feel confident about the flying lessons, while the other sign made you run in terror.

When you have the right stimulus, it's easier to change behavior, motivate action, or just plain win someone's heart. But it has to be both specific to your needs and *subtle*. A full-frontal attack usually fails, because it just causes your subject to dig his heels in and resist you. This is especially important to remember when you are dealing with alpha males. They do not respond well to being told what to do. They will, however, respond to the right stimulus.

Another lesson that Stimulus/Response teaches is that everything you do sends a signal. Like the way you dress if you are a woman. For instance: if you wear pants instead of dresses, or whether your skirts are too short or too long. Your shoes send a signal about you, as does your hairstyle, the *length* of your hair, the color of your hair, whether you wear makeup or not, and how much makeup you wear. Everything marks you, and people form an opinion about you based on how you execute your image. Just like those signs. So think about what you want your image to be and what response you want people to have when they meet you for the first time.

The "Blind Man Story" below is a famous example of Stimulus/Response combined with emotional advertising. We all use this story with clients, because it makes us feel that our skills at persuasion can be used for the greater good instead of just for selling cornflakes. I don't know for certain who originated this story, but we think it was Charles Saatchi. It also involves a sign.

The Blind Man Story: A blind man sits at a corner on Madison Avenue in New York City. He is holding an empty cup and a sign that says *"I am blind. Please help me."* But no one does. A lot of busy people look at him and walk right past him without putting even a quarter in his cup. Then an advertising man comes along and notices that the blind man's sign is not altering anyone's behavior. He offers to rewrite the sign, and when he does, everything changes. People stop, read the sign, and put *folded* money into the man's cup. The blind man asks, "What did you write on my sign?" And the adman says, *"Today is the first day of spring. And I am blind."*

Here are some examples of Stimulus/Response that manipulate without malice. The first time I used this intuitively was with my ex-husband.

PROBLEM: My first husband, the crabby actor, was raised in an old-fashioned Sicilian household, where the women did all the work and were actually slaves to the men. As a result of this upbringing, he didn't help with any of the housework in our marriage. It wasn't because he didn't *want* to do it; he just *couldn't* do it. It was too emasculating for him. But I worked a full-time job and still did all the cooking and cleaning. When I asked him to help, it turned into an argument, and he still wouldn't lend a hand. After a while I was so tired, I tried a different tactic.

SOLUTION: I bought a super-duper vacuum cleaner that was also very heavy and hard to drag around. After a week of using it, I told him I was going to return it because I couldn't manage it—I just wasn't strong enough. He was eager to show me that he was. For the last two years of our marriage, he did all the vacuuming, and toward the end, he actually cooked dinner once or twice. I had used the right stimulus with a little feminine vulnerability thrown in for good measure.

I use this winning combination with men in business all the time. I play on their masculine pride and natural instincts to protect the "weaker" sex.

"I can't figure this out, and I'm exhausted," I will say to one of the men at the office. "And if it's not done by tomorrow, I'm dead."

"I'll do it," he'll invariably say.

But his rescue mission won't be truly satisfying to him unless I show appreciation for the sacrifice he is making on my behalf. This is as crucial as saying thank you.

"No, no, you're swamped, too," I'll say.

"I'll make the time for it."

"Thank you. I love you."

"I know. You're welcome."

It's like great sex. Everyone walks away feeling fulfilled.

PROBLEM: I was having an issue with one of the senior account managers when I was a group creative director at McCann. No matter what creative we did for his clients, he had a problem with it. Sometimes he couldn't even articulate what was wrong with an idea—he just didn't like it. It wasn't his idea, and he wouldn't support it in front of the client who thought he hung the moon.

SOLUTION: Let him hold the copy. I thought if he had some ownership for an idea, he would be its champion. So I would bring him in to the process at the earliest stage. I did what creative people hate the most: I let him see rough ideas before they were fully crafted. It was risky, but it paid off. I listened to his comments early on, and it was simple enough to guide him toward the best ideas. He always defended them to the hilt when he took them to his clients. This seems like a logical move now, but in the late eighties, creative directors just didn't collaborate with people who weren't "creative"—like account managers or even clients. I'm not sure many of them do it even now.

PROBLEM: I was almost ready to be hired as the creative director for the J. Walter Thompson Chicago office, but I had to have a meeting with Jim Patterson, who was the worldwide chief creative officer for JWT. This was before he became James Patterson, one of the best-read novelists in the world (*Kiss the Girls, Along Came a Spider*). I had to prove to this man who didn't know me from Adam that I was the perfect candidate to bring the declining Chicago office back to life.

SOLUTION: We decided to meet over lunch, which meant I would have about an hour to position myself as the best and strongest candidate for the job. Jim had a full beard in those days, and the lobster-salad sandwich he had ordered was full of mayonnaise that was getting all over his beard. I sweetly pointed out to him that he would need a shower when we were finished with lunch, and did he notice how neat *my* lunch was? Neat and clean. "I've out-ordered you," I said to him. "Want my napkin?" The next day, Jim was interviewed by *New York Times* advertising columnist Stuart Elliott, who had devoted his entire column to my move to Chicago. Jim's great quote was that I was "the most competitive person, man or woman" he'd met. "But in a positive way, the way you would talk about a Michael Jordan or a Larry Bird wanting to win."

PROBLEM: Stimulus/Response is such a powerful psychological tool, it even works with animals. My husband and I own horses. One of them was eating too much grass and was getting fat. This is dangerous for some breeds and can lead to foundering or lamini-tis, a frightening condition that comes on fast and is often fatal. It became necessary to put a grazing mask on her to force her to eat our rich grass slowly instead of gorging on it. But she hated the mask. My goal was to get her to love it.

SOLUTION: Every time I put her mask on her, I would drop four of her beloved Mrs. Pastures Cookies for Horses inside the mask so she could munch on them while I attached the feeding muzzle around her head. Now she associates the mask with her cookies and practically puts the mask on herself. Thank you, Dr. Pavlov.

The lesson learned here is that most living things can be trained if the motivation is there and the rewards are obvious. Unpleasant tasks are more agreeable when there is even a small amount of pleasure attached to them. This works with animals, children, and the people with whom you work. It's just common sense, and it works like a charm with men. Yet I am constantly amazed at how many intelligent women either don't understand this concept or refuse to manipulate a situation. Testosterone is too powerful for us to handle with reason and intellect alone. And it comes at us in too many shapes, sizes, and flavors. There's an overpowering amount of testosterone in all men, whether they are alpha males or not.

3

Gentlemen vs. Hooligans

When we are young and attractive, we walk a precarious line with men. Our attempts to be seen as equals can lead to the wrong assumptions on their part. If we are too much like "one of the guys," we run the risk of inviting unwanted advances or other forms of disrespect. If we are too protective of our sensibilities, we run the risk of being seen as too prissy. Either way, someone ends up uncomfortable. And if you work in a boys club, a man's discomfort can hold you back. We have to navigate our way through their clubs' regulations and strike a balance between respect and acceptance. It's a difficult, delicate tightrope we walk, and the women who get this right can win big.

So what are the pitfalls? The most damaging one is seemingly the most innocent: laughter. What could be wrong with making someone laugh, right? But when we are young and vulnerable, we have to be careful about what we find funny. Sometimes humor is used as a weapon against us, to belittle us, embarrass us, or simply "show us who is boss." There are some men who are threatened by women with a powerful presence, and while you're on your way up, they will try to take you down. An easy way·for them to hurt you is with humiliation.

When I decided to leave the sheltered halls of the ultimate gentlemens club (Young & Rubicam) to go to the rowdy boys club of McCann Erickson, I developed terminal hives. Welts the size of pillows covered my body for an entire week, and wearing clothes became torture. When the lower half of my face puffed out like a football, I sought medical help. A series of cortisone shots finally got the inflammation under control. I was told that if the hives had traveled to my throat, I could have suffocated. As in dying. It seems my body knew instinctively that I had much to fear in making the transition from working with gentlemen to working with hooligans. My body turned out to be right.

I arrived at McCann on February 9, 1987. I was brought in as one of four senior vice president/group creative directors in a newly reorganized creative department. John Nieman, the new executive creative director of McCann New York and the man who had been my boss at Y&R, hired me. I was the only female group creative director in this new creative department and the first woman to have this title at McCann.

I had three strikes against me from the start.

Strike one: I was an outsider. The other· three men had been given their group creative director positions with battlefield commissions, as they had been at McCann for a while. They knew where all the bodies were buried and had even buried a few of those bodies themselves.

Strike two: Coming from Young & Rubicam, I soon discovered there was an intense rivalry between McCann and Y&R. McCann thought the people at Young & Rubicam were effete snobs who based their success wholly on their personal relationships with clients, not performance. Y&R referred to McCann as a company of hooligans, bullies, and philistines.

My very first meeting at McCann made it clear that I was

viewed as a Y&R wimp. I was the only woman in a group of men who were violently disagreeing with one another. At Y&R, this kind of conflict would have been handled with gentle diplomacy:

"I see where you're going with your line of reasoning, Elliott, but let me point out a few things that might change your mind."

Then everyone would listen politely, and if they were still in disagreement, they would engage in a quiet, respectful debate.

But at McCann it was handled this way:

"WHAT THE FUCK ARE YOU TALKING ABOUT, HENRY?"

And they wouldn't even wait for someone to finish a sentence before they attacked. (Even now at McCann we interrupt one another when absolutely essential. We know it's a disgusting habit and we're working on it. For instance, now when we interrupt someone, we say "sorry" while we are doing it. Hey, it's a start.)

When I first arrived at McCann, however, this rowdy behavior floored me. For one thing, I had never heard the word *fuck* used in a business meeting before. Even the creative people I knew who tended to use colorful language would say things like "frigging" or "freaking" or some other euphemism for the F-word, especially in a meeting. My face must have turned white at that outburst, because one of the men turned to me with a big grin.

"What's the matter?" he asked. "Your gentlemen friends at Y&R don't say 'fuck'? Bunch of wimps."

The third strike against me wasn't my fault either: I was a woman. I felt sure that the other three male group creative directors resented me, as did most of the people in the creative department. My fears were confirmed when I saw my new office on the day I arrived. The good news was that it was a large office. The bad news was that it was at the end of a deserted hallway, and it was filled, *filled,* with all of the unwanted desks, chairs, and credenzas from the creative department. They had given me the office they used for storing excess furniture.

Then I met the twenty-two writers and art directors who had been assigned to my group. Instead of firing the people who were either too difficult or too untalented, they just gave them all to me. Now I had unwanted furniture and unwanted creative people. It took me only a couple of weeks to realize that, of my twenty-two writers and art directors, only a handful were going to help me do great work. Then it took me almost a year to fire the people who didn't belong there and bring in the creative talent I needed to run the one good business I had been assigned: the blue-chip account of AT&T Business-to-Business. (I did have one other good account in Premium Saltines, Nabisco's biggest-selling cracker, but it wouldn't take up any of my time because Nabisco didn't support Premium Saltines with advertising. It literally sold itself.)

Whatever the reason, I became the unwilling audience for a lot of male humor. The worst offender was one of the group creative directors, who took great pleasure in making me squirm. Let's call him Chuck, because, like Charles Bronson, he had a rugged look that was attractive in a brutish kind of way. His favorite pastime was describing sexual acts to me involving men and gerbils. And he always did it when he had an audience of other men around us. I'd be walking down the hall, and he'd rush out of his office with a magazine.

"Nina, Nina. C'mere."

He always had his posse of young creative guys nearby, and they would materialize out of thin air whenever he needed a handy audience.

"What is it?"

"Listen to this." And he would proceed to describe how gerbils were used for anal sex.

"You're disgusting," I'd say, and then I'd flounce off to my office and slam the door. But that just gave him bigger laughs.

Most of the time he would tell jokes in poor taste and I would just ignore him. But that was not working either.

He was winning the war.

Then I developed a better tactic. When he told a disgusting joke, I would laugh just *before* he delivered the punch line. Or—and this *killed* him—I would laugh right *on* the punch line. That annoyed him so much, he stopped telling jokes in front of me entirely. It wasn't fun for him anymore, but it had become a real hoot for me.

I'd like to say that Chuck got his comeuppance and suffered greatly for his cruelty to me, but in fact he never did. I had to figure out how to diffuse his aggressive behavior toward me all by myself. What could I do, I thought, to change his attitude? If I wanted his respect and friendship, what stimulus did I need to win him over? Once I figured out his Achilles' heel, it was easy.

As with all men, and creative people especially, the ego is the root of all vulnerability. I know two things about creative people: First, we are constantly trying to win the respect of other creative people, and we never stop trying to impress our peers with our creative genius; and second, it's a well-known fact that clients rarely buy our best work. In fact, some clients are gifted "shit-sniffers." If you have a terrible idea buried in a pile of great work, they will sniff out the crappy idea and buy that one.

Armed with these two insights, I would stop by Chuck's office when we were working late and no one else was around to drool over the storyboards he couldn't sell to his clients. (All creative people keep their dead ideas around so everyone will know we are not hacks, and the terrible work we produce is the clients' fault.) I would tell him that a client was crazy and his work would have won him a Gold Lion at Cannes (the highest creative award in the universe). I would spend hours with him while he pulled out all of the brilliant ideas that never sold and acted them out for me while puffing on a joint.

All of his dead work was very funny, even though some of it was inappropriate for the clients he was working for. I didn't care. I laughed and drooled over him like a moron. After a few weeks, he relaxed and stopped trying to "get" me. He started coming into my office when he had a good idea, and I would tell him he was brilliant. In time, he decided that my taste in creative was flawless, and that I was brilliant, too. I actually grew to like the scoundrel. He eventually left McCann and started his own agency. Today he's very successful.

But the bad boys at McCann paled in comparison to the testosterone-laden culture that was waiting for me at my first job as agency creative director. After almost five years as a group creative director at McCann, I was given a chance to break out of the sea of other GCDs in New York.

J. Walter Thompson was looking for an executive creative director for its Chicago outpost, and I was one of the candidates on its list. I had known all along that if I wanted to reach my ultimate goal—running the creative department of a large New York agency—I might have to leave town as a stepping-stone. Leaving McCann would be a hardship for me, but I also knew that if the opportunity came my way, I would have to take it. I was pumped.

But then I got cancer.

Damn.

There's nothing like breast cancer to put a damper on things.

In June of 1991, three different surgeons told me I was lucky. If I let them remove my left breast, there would probably be no need for chemotherapy or radiation, and I probably wouldn't have to worry about breast cancer anymore. I went to two more doctors, both women. I thought they might be more breast-sensitive. But they all said the same thing. A month later, one of the four performed a mastectomy, and it turned out they were all correct in their diagnosis. It was clean and simple. No chemotherapy or radiation. But still, it was my left breast. My favorite one.

NOTE: *I can't emphasize enough how important it is to have a mammogram once a year if you are thirty-five or older. My cancer was not a lump. The cancer cells were in my milk ducts, virtually undetectable except to X-rays. Without a mammogram, there would have been no way to detect this cancer until it had metastasized throughout my body. By then treatment would have been too late. Don't ignore your body. And don't use your career as an excuse to miss doctor appointments.*

In preparing for my mastectomy, I had to get past my grief quickly. After all, I was a busy person. Steve Davis, the new general manager of JWT Chicago, was zeroing in on me as a prime candidate to be his creative partner, and every other week I was having a meal with him. Most of the time he would come to New York, but once or twice I had to fly to Chicago.

Also, by this time, I was running a larger creative group at McCann with a lot more business. During the previous five years I had been given all of the cracker business in Nabisco's lineup (Ritz, Ritz Bits, Wheat Thins, and Triscuits—Saltines still wasn't advertising). I also had Alka-Seltzer by this time and my beloved AT&T. Now more than thirty people in my group needed my attention.

I had to figure out what would make me feel better about such a devastating physical loss so I could get on with my life. At times like this, I played the "hey, it could be worse" game based on the assumption that no matter what catastrophe befalls you, it could always be worse. I told myself that of all the things I had in pairs—eyes, ears, legs, arms, lungs—losing a breast was the smallest hardship. It would also be the easiest to replace.

All of this was happening in between my dinner dates with Steve Davis. And it definitely felt as if I were dating this tall, attractive, smooth operator. Never in the history of western civilization had anyone taken so long to hire a creative director; Steve searched for almost a year.

The creative director's job is the most influential position at an ad agency, and it's almost preferable to have *no* creative director than the wrong one. This person can either make or break an ad agency. He manages the entire creative department and influences every single person at the agency. He is responsible for all of the creative work that the agency does, as well as the business results for all of the clients. He is also the key to bringing in new business. (Notice I keep saying "he"?) The executive creative director's job is the most dangerous one in the ad business, because the failure rate is high and failure is easily identified; it's also very public and unforgiving. Who could blame Steve for trying so hard to make the right decision?

I didn't want him to know I was having a mastectomy. I didn't want to give him any reason to move me off the top of his list, and I was sure I was in first place. He didn't have *time* to feed any other candidate the way he was feeding me and still run his Chicago agency. Later I found out that I was right. Although he met with everyone in the business that could possibly do the job, he didn't feed any of them as much as he fed me.

In between our "dates" I had my mastectomy. Two weeks after the surgery, Steve offered me the job and I accepted. Two weeks after that—with an enormous pain in my chest where my left breast used to be—I packed my bags and moved to Chicago to become the latest in a string of New York creative directors for JWT's Midwest office.

And that leads to another good question. Why leave a good job where you are happy and safe and take one that scares the hell out of you? Because that's what you have to do if you are trying to get to the top. A secure and comfortable job only holds you back. If you want to make a name for yourself, find a mess and fix it. Find something that looks so impossibly beyond repair that fixing it will earn the respect and admiration of everyone. The more visible the mess is, the more dangerous, but if you succeed . . . *you will be a hero!* When given the opportunity, always go after a turnaround. If you join a successful company, you'll still have to work hard to make it even more successful, but it's less of a marvel. There is something very exciting about taking a job where others have failed, especially if those others were all men.

Chicago was notorious for annihilating creative directors from New York. The town just chewed them up and spit them out. It was clear that everyone in the ad industry would be watching my every move, because here was yet another New York asshole heading west. It was even juicier with me because this New York asshole was a *woman.* I took the job with a lot of fanfare in *The New York Times* and trade publications such as *Advertising Age* and *Adweek.* Success would make me famous. If I failed, I would be infamous, but for a shorter period of time, like a day or two.

While a good turnaround opportunity can build your reputation quickly, it has to be the perfect bowl of porridge: not too hot, not too cold, not too big, not too small. The company has to be in trouble, but not so far gone that it's a lost cause. It has to be important, or at least important enough for people to care whether it survives or not. It has to be large enough to make a blip on everyone's radar screen, but not so big as to make your task impossible. It has to be just right.

JWT's Chicago office was perfect for me. Once the jewel in the J. Walter Thompson crown, it had suffered one major setback after another, and yet the ad community was on its side. Everyone wanted this shop to succeed. But by 1991, a string of autocratic men from New York had come and gone. Their answer to Chicago's woes was to stop losing business and start winning again. But no one gave the people in that office the confidence they needed to be winners again, and no one offered a blueprint for success. With each new "agent of change," more business was lost, morale plummeted, the good people left, and the hangers-on clung even tighter for dear life.

As the latest general manager from New York, Steve Davis was aware of the fear and distrust in Chicago, and he wanted his creative director/partner to help him nurture the place back to good health. He knew that the people in the office needed someone who was tough enough to help lead them but nurturing enough to do it without crushing their spirit. They needed someone who could deal with their boys club mentality but was patient enough to guide them, sometimes without their cooperation. They needed support, some genuine affection, and the tools to become winners again. In short: They needed a good woman. Actually, they needed a mom—someone who would recognize their potential, build up their confidence, and care for them unconditionally.

The saddest part of the decline of that Chicago office was the history of its accomplishments. The brilliant positioning of 7-Up as the "Uncola" in the seventies came out of this office, as did the branding of Oscar Mayer, with unforgettable songs like "Oh, I Wish I Was an Oscar Mayer Wiener" and "My Bologna Has a First Name." At one point, Chicago had more billings than the New York office, and it was widely believed that this was the basis for the friction between the two offices: deep-seated jealousy.

But by the mid-1980s, Chicago was rapidly declining. The once-glorious shop, which had billed more than $700 million in the seventies and eighties, was down to less than $250 million when I walked through the doors of this turbo-charged boys club. I don't know if the place had hit rock bottom—that's always a subjective judgment—but no one could argue that we had a long way to bounce back up. Now the people in charge wanted Steve Davis and me—two more New Yorkers—to turn the place around and make it a jewel once more. But there is always a good reason for a string of failures. When you walk into a place with that pattern, make sure you don't get blown up before the battle even starts. I had a plan of action: mainly, to watch my step.

Find the Minefields and Don't Step on Any

When you join a company with a wounded soul and a culture that is alien to you, everyone is a potential threat to your success. If you're a woman coming to save a boys club, it's even more hazardous. You have no idea who your enemies are, or if you have any supporters at all. Everyone will be willing to talk to you, but you won't have a clear idea of whom to trust. I suggest that you take everything with a huge grain of salt. There is very little you can depend on, but you can always count on the following:

There will never be enough time in the day to attend to everything you thought needed your attention when you woke up that morning. This will never change as long as you are in charge.

Everyone will have his or her own agenda. The good people will be jockeying for a better position, and the losers will be looking for places to continue hiding. Be wary of your instant supporters, as they are either the best or the worst of the bunch, and it might not be clear which is which. Some really good people may decide to throw their support your way until you prove unworthy. Some really bad people who show instant love may be frightened of losing their jobs. Some of the real talent might be somewhat unapproachable. They will be arrogantly secure and expect you to make overtures to them. You will have to prove your worth to this group. Find out who these people are, swallow your pride, then take the first step and reach out to them.

There will be some people who will have loved your predecessor, and they will resent you. Others will have hated him and be more inclined to accept you. At first, you may not recognize the difference between resistance and acceptance, especially if you are in a repressed culture or a Midwestern company filled with passive-aggressive personalities.

Talk to as many people as you can, but listen to the ones who have nothing to gain or lose. I always befriend the secretaries, for instance. They are generally a good source for honesty, and they rarely have a secret agenda or ax to grind. If they have been at the company for a long time, they will have seen a lot of big shots come and go. Find out what they think without delving into gossip. Also, talk to the people who are close to retirement; they have already had their careers and have no reason to lie to you. In any event, make up your own mind.

I had an inkling of what the Chicago office was feeling and thinking, but I had no idea what the actual environment was like. I discovered a place that was drunk on testosterone. There was a lot of old-school, Chicago ad-guy posturing for positions of power, and male chauvinism permeated the halls—a residue from the previous leadership. There was no doubt in anyone's mind that a female creative director was threatening to most if not all of them. Few people are ever glad to see a female leader. We have to prove ourselves every step of the way.

The macho environment at JWT/Chicago was encouraged and crafted by the previous two men who ran the office. One of them kept a hand grenade on his desk and, when looking at creative work, liked to remark, "I'm fascinated . . . and I'm repelled." (I thought it was funny when I heard it, but the other people in the office didn't.) The other macho man was the creative director (let's call him Sammy), who singled out a few favorite disciples and didn't have much patience for the rest of his creative group. He never fired any of these unwanted people, he just ignored them and kept hiring other people to do the kind of work he valued. Together, these two alpha males created a tremendous need for someone like me. It's always easier to follow a leader with perceived flaws than one who is allegedly perfect.

One of the few creative people who didn't appear to hate me on sight was a young, talented writer named Gib Marquardt. He wasn't exactly a supporter; he just hadn't decided whether or not to resent me. Gib, a six-foot-two-inch blond, blue-eyed ex–hockey player, recently described the tone of the office when I arrived:

"It was an all-male high-school fraternity," Gib said. "Very cliquey, very intimidating. If you weren't *like* [the creative director], he didn't like *you.* In the wake of the chaos this leadership created, in walks this chick from New York, Ms. DiSesa, who tried to get us all to put aside our manly, destructive ways, to get in touch with our female sides—whatever that meant—and support one another instead of fighting."

As confusing as I was to them, there was only one of me for them to contend with. I had a horde of angry men to deal with and they *all* baffled me.

Remember That Nothing Is Inexplicable

Every single person in the Chicago office was a stranger to me, and I couldn't second-guess anyone's actions. Sometimes the staff's behavior seemed irrational, a concept I don't believe in. Every action and prejudice, every emotional outburst has a logical reason behind it. If something doesn't make sense, it's because the complete backstory is missing. Find out exactly what has happened to provoke the conduct you see, and then piece it all together with possible scenarios. It's like solving a murder mystery. Collect the clues, lay them all out, and you will solve the puzzle.

The most confounding group of any agency I have ever worked in is always the creative people. They present a unique challenge to everyone, especially the young, inexperienced account managers who believe they are put on this earth to give creative minds some discipline. (They are always much happier once they outgrow this obsession.)

Once a young account manager came to see me in a fury. It seemed that the most senior creative person on his business had just screamed bloody murder at him and then threw him out of his office. And it wasn't the first time this had happened either.

I told the account manager that when creative people "lose it," it's usually because we are frightened. Our biggest fears revolve around either some kind of creative breakdown, like when we can't think of an idea, or Public Humiliation, where we *have* an idea, we realize it might possibly suck, and we have no time to improve on it or think of something else. Evidently, the account manager was doing something that scared the creative guy.

"Find out what that is," I said, "and then stop doing it."

"I didn't do anything," the account guy told me. "I didn't *say* anything. He just started screaming at me as soon as I walked in his office."

"What was he screaming at you?"

" *'Get the fuck out of my office!'* "

"What were you doing there in the first place?"

At first there was just silence. Then he confessed:

"I go there every day and give him our job status sheets to remind him when everything is due."

We stared at each other. The young account guy's eyes were round saucers waiting for the pearls of wisdom from my lips that would solve all of his problems. So I told him to do a status check with the creative people just once a week and stop adding more pressure to an already tense job.

"Trust me," I said, "he knows all the jobs that are due. You're just making him crazier than he already is."

Creative people are always insecure and scared that they won't come up with their next big idea in time for their next deadline. They don't need to be reminded of that every single day by young, overzealous account managers.

Why Saviors Are Crucified

You would think that when you come charging in on your white horse, people would be glad to see you. Not so. It is not gratifying to play the role of savior; you have to learn that and then manage your expectations. The people you have come to rescue are rarely waiting to greet you with open arms. They will not be happy to admit failure, and they will be terrified that you are going to fire them for no good reason, just to make room for your own people.

Most companies don't bring in leaders from the outside unless they are in serious trouble and are looking for a miracle worker. Under normal circumstances, they like to promote from within, because it shows stability and confidence in the team. This gave the men in the Chicago creative department two reasons to dislike me. It meant that none of them were good enough for the top job . . . but a *woman* was, and one from *New York,* no less. That Second City paranoia kicks in even more so when we come to their town to be the boss.

This notion became crystal clear to me on that first day on the job, when my impassioned and inspiring speech was met with Tim Kane's wise-guy remark.

"Any questions?" I asked.

"What's your sign?"

Those three simple words issued a sweeping and complicated challenge, and there couldn't have been a clearer signal sent. All the irreverence, arrogance, resistance, and bad behavior that was waiting for me in Chicago was summed up brilliantly in those three words.

"What's your sign?"

From that day forward, and for the next three years, Tim Kane and Dean Bastian, along with their gang of creative bad boys, would be the bane of my existence in my attempt to bring JWT/Chicago up to snuff.

4

The Bad Boys on 27

The second indication that Tim Kane and his incorrigible group were going to be trouble was geography. While the rest of the creative department, including myself, worked on the twenty-sixth floor at 900 N. Michigan Ave., the Bad Boys had commandeered the twenty-seventh floor, and they ruled with terror.

They were my biggest challenge as the new executive creative director, and it didn't take me long to realize that I needed that rowdy bunch of guys who weren't inclined to change their ways. It's not clear how Tim and Dean hired for their group, but most of these young men mirrored their bosses. They were talented, overly confident, and not programmed to listen to me. They were also very attractive, and yet, the young women in the office dreaded making a trip to their floor. It was considered a hazardous duty.

When the Bad Boys got bored, they would play catch in the hallways, and anyone who interfered with their game—for instance, by trying to walk down the hall—did so at his or her own risk. At first I thought they weren't very good at playing catch, because their balls frequently went wild and they were constantly breaking the light fixtures on the walls. Then it dawned on me: They were *aiming* at the light fixtures, but they just kept missing them. Either way, their aim was terrible. I pointed this out to them:

"You stink at this. Why don't you just go and make some ads? Maybe you'll be better at that."

Smirks.

The Bad Boys included Gib Marquardt and his metrosexual partner, Paul Behnen, who looked like a younger version of Calvin Klein; Joe Burke, handsome and too charming for his own good; Michael Rivera, young and in training as a heartbreaker; and Phil Schneider, a funny, quirky guy who did strange things like hide his underwear behind the door in his office. I once asked him why he did that.

"It's not underwear," he said, "it just looks like underwear."

I waited for a further explanation, but he had already distracted himself with a Rubik's Cube. Another time Phil took a Polaroid of his fiancée sitting on the toilet with a hangover, and then shared it with the whole agency. She still married him.

I was surprised to see two very sweet and talented young women in this bad-boy gang: Dawn Dingman and Melissa Storch. They were the only women the Bad Boys didn't torment or intimidate. I guess Dawn and Melissa "belonged" to them, and the guys were very protective of these women, in a big-brother sort of way. This actually gave me hope that the Bad Boys might be salvageable. By the time I left JWT, I was thankful I hadn't killed them all in their sleep. I had wanted to do that at the very beginning.

One of the exceptions in this group was Dave Moore, a brown-haired Kiefer Sutherland clone (he even sounds like him). Although Dave was as talented and therefore as stubborn as the rest of the Bad Boys, he came into the agency during my watch and was therefore more inclined to listen to me. He wouldn't necessarily follow my advice, but he would at least appear to be listening.

Initially, Tim and Dean had been talking to Dave for a while about joining the agency, but Dave was happy where he was (at Leo Burnett) and didn't want to leave his job. He recently recalled the day he finally agreed to take the job at J. Walter Thompson:

"I was firm about staying at Burnett, and then you came to Thompson," Dave said. "One day I was back talking to Tim and Dean again. I must have had my book* out, because you passed by, sized up the situation immediately, and with a huge grin yelled at me from the doorway, '*Don't do it!*' I'm sure you don't remember that incident, but I will remember it forever. You had me at 'Don't.' "

Except for Dave, all of the Bad Boys on 27 had a previous relationship with Steve Davis, and they felt protected by him. They'd been without a creative leader for almost a year and had gotten used to the idea of Steve being their "real" boss. Given the life expectancy of agency creative directors in general, I'm sure they also assumed that I would be gone soon enough. My brilliant plan was to thwart that assumption.

I used a variety of strategies with the Bad Boys at the beginning of our undeclared war, including everything I'd learned about handling creative people and men in particular. But every tactic to win them over and control them appeared to fail—subtlety especially. They needed a heavier hand and a major dose of seduction and manipulation.

First, I tried out-and-out bribery.

The Bad Boys wanted a "beer room" where they could hang out. They said their creative juices would thrive better in a more "creative" environment. I found the money in my paltry budget to rent a pool table, so we turned one of their conference rooms into a pool hall. That room was right above my corner office on the

---

* A creative person's book, or portfolio, is an assemblage of the best creative work that he or she has done. Its sole purpose is to help creative people get their next job. The book and the interview are the entire hiring process.

twenty-sixth floor, and as a way of showing their gratitude, they would bang their pool cues on the floor to annoy me. And it did.

The creative people who worked on the twenty-sixth floor wanted to know where *their* pool table was.

"Walk upstairs," I told them.

"Can't," they said. "Not allowed."

I told Tim and Dean that they had to allow everyone to play, that the pool hall was not for their private use. I got blank stares and innocent assurances that everyone was welcome. But the twenty-sixth floor still felt unloved, and I felt compelled to buy them a Ping-Pong table (with my own money) and set it up in an empty office. One day I went into the Ping-Pong room to play and saw that someone had punched a hole in the wall the size of a *tire*. Is that what it's like to have sons, I thought?

Next I tried food. Food is love, right? I took everyone in the group out to lunch individually, and told them how important they were to the agency and to me. I shared my game plan to make the agency shine again. I said that with their help, we could grow and add the kinds of clients that would buy the great work I knew they all wanted to do. I wanted fame and fortune for us all. But what did *they* want? The two young women, Melissa and Dawn, were very thoughtful about their deepest desires regarding their careers and potential growth as creative people, and they willingly shared those goals with me.

The men didn't have a plan. Tim and Dean thought about it for a while and decided that what they really *needed* was a speedboat.

And the abhorrent behavior continued. In desperation, I tried violence. I bought a high-powered water rifle, and when they misbehaved by banging their pool cues on my ceiling, breaking the light fixtures in the halls, or terrorizing the young women, I would march up to the twenty-seventh floor and blast them with water. But we all enjoyed that a little too much, and it didn't change anything.

I tried befriending them. Getting down to their level. Gib recently reminded me of one time in particular.

"We were an immature and rough bunch back then," he said, stating the obvious. "That you were willing to wade into our world and even participate in the general grab-ass nature of things earned you a hell of a lot of respect. I remember how drunk you got with us one time drinking shots of Jägermeister in competition with Dave, even though Dean kept advising you to pace yourself. We sent you home in a taxi at eight-thirty that night. Christ, it was still *light* out, and we'd only just gotten to the bar at eight o'clock. Your husband was so mad at us. You were Mom, but you were Cool Mom, and we were the unruly teens feeling our oats. You gave us a lot of rope to do that."

Speaking of that husband, it was a small miracle that I'd had the time or energy to fall in love. Everything I did was focused on saving JWT/Chicago. The only man I was dating was this guy named Brian Goodall. I had been hearing about him for the previous five years in New York from my McCann boss and friend, John Nieman. Every time I was between men, I'd ask John if he knew any single men, and he'd always say, "My friend Brian Goodall. In Chicago." They had been best friends since they were twenty-two and both working at their first advertising agency in St. Louis. I was sure Brian would be a great guy, but it was still a long way to go for dinner and a drink. Then, several years before my move to Chicago, Brian and I were introduced to each other. It was at a Super Bowl party in New York at the house of our mutual friend and matchmaker. It was meant to be The Big Meeting for us.

After all those years of hearing about each other, our only exchange at this party was:

"So you're Brian Goodall."

"Uh-huh."

For the rest of the day, Brian totally ignored me. Truly, he did not say one word to me, and it wasn't because he was enthralled with the game. I found out later that he didn't even like football. He sat right next to me in John's living room and taught John's twelve-month-old son how to tear pages out of a magazine. What a putz. Naturally, I hated him.

I didn't see Brian again until three years later. Right around the time Steve Davis was talking to me about J. Walter Thompson, Brian was also looking for an executive creative director for an agency where he was general manager—a highly respected shop named Bayer Bess Vanderwalker.

He took me to lunch in Manhattan. It was March 14, 1991. I remember that day clearly, because the day before I had gotten those painfully dumb collagen injections in my lips, to plump them up, and I'd had a bad reaction. Instead of having sexy bee-stung lips, my whole mouth was swollen and puffed up. If I drank from a glass, the liquid would dribble down my chin.

Rob McKinley, a man with whom I worked very closely, was ready with the quick, insightful, and helpful advice he was known for giving.

"Jesus," he said. "Don't let him see you in profile. You look like one of those Ubangi women."

"Thanks."

"And drink through a *straw*, for Christ's sake."

The job with Brian's agency never materialized, and I didn't see him again until I moved to Chicago five months later to take the JWT job. But I got even with Mr. Goodall. I married him on May 23, 1992, just fourteen months after that Ubangi-lip lunch and nine months after I arrived in Chicago.

That showed him a thing or two.

The Impact of Schadenfreude

The Germans have a word for what I found at JWT: "Schadenfreude." It means the pleasure one derives from someone else's misfortune. This is valuable when you are competing against an outsider, but it's not helpful when people in the same company, and especially on the same team, feel this way about each other.

Chicago's operating system was steeped in deriving pleasure from the misfortunes of others, because the ones who were left standing improved their positions in the food chain. The intense politics of that office were suffocating, and the pockets of power impenetrable. Since there had been a steady stream of new leadership every year, the only job security people had was with the power of a client relationship. When I got there, information was a source of that power, and no one shared anything with anyone else. It was literally every man for himself.

As a result, there was a lot of destructive competition throughout the office. I tried to encourage people to save their aggression for our competitors but had little success. It wasn't in their nature. Somehow, I had to *inspire* them to see things my way. I needed to use my female talents and skills at benevolent manipulation in order to help them behave better.

Death by Innuendo

Most of the damage that the turf-protectors at JWT inflicted on one another was through innuendo, not outright attacks. It's hard to defend yourself against this subtle but effective type of slander. Unlike at McCann, where people would stab you in the chest so you could see it coming, in Chicago it was generally a blade in the back when you least expected it.

Death by Innuendo was regrettably easy to execute. For instance, if any one of my lieutenants in the creative department wanted to discredit me with a client, they could do it swiftly and invisibly anytime they showed that client creative ideas in my absence. If the client hated one idea in particular, my would-be assassin might slip in the blade:

"Oh gee," they might say. "That was Nina's favorite." If they did it enough times, I'd be dead meat with that client and wouldn't even know why. They could also drop subtle hints that indicated I was out of touch with a client's business. It could happen at lunch, on the phone, on the golf course, or at any other time when I was not present. You can see how an enterprising account manager or creative person who has the client's ear can poison the well. If a head account manager wanted to diffuse the authority of a group creative director, there were ample opportunities to be a silent killing machine. Death by Innuendo rarely failed.

Although this hadn't happened to me yet, it was only a matter of time before it did. I knew I couldn't *enforce* loyalty; it had to come willingly. The people in that office had to want to protect and defend me, but how was I going to get them to do that when they didn't even want to support one another? I couldn't fire everyone who behaved badly—there were too many of them, and half of them didn't report to me—so I tried to manipulate them all into being better people.

First I would squelch the negative and share the positive.

For instance, I would be in a meeting with Ed Jones, and he'd say:

"Jack Smith is an ass."

"Really?" I'd say, with great surprise. "Jack's an ass? Because just yesterday he was saying what a good brief *you* wrote for the XYZ client."

But what Jack had *actually* said about Ed was:

"The brief Ed wrote is good, but believe me, that's the only thing he ever does well. He's an idiot savant."

Faint praise, but praise nonetheless. So all I did was pass on an edited version of Jack's comment—"The brief Ed wrote is good." I left out the whole second half, especially the idiot savant crack. I'm not exactly lying when I do this; I'm just not telling the whole truth. This is allowed under my personal code of ethics.

Now Ed Jones has a decision to make. He can continue to dump on Jack and thereby render anything good Jack said about *him* as meaningless. Or he could try to soften his own insult.

"Jack liked that brief?" Ed says. "It *was* damn good." Ed is puffing up right before my eyes.

"Well, sometimes Jack's an ass," Ed says, "and sometimes he shows good judgment." Ed can't help it. He feels proud that someone who doesn't like him still thinks he did a good job. That's a big compliment, because it doesn't have an agenda. A compliment given begrudgingly is the most sincere kind.

The next time Jack dumped on Ed I would say, "You know, Jack, Ed Jones told his whole group the other day what good judgment you have." (He did sort of say that.) And now *Jack* would puff up like a peacock.

When someone said something good about another person, I would pass it along. When they said something bad, I would say, "Really? He just told me yesterday how smart *you* are." After a while (and it felt like an eternity) people gradually started to resent one another less. At least they stopped attacking one another in front of me. The ones who never got with the program we transferred to another office, or another agency. Saintly patience only goes so far.

As Machiavellian as these tactics were, I was really aiming for a more nurturing environment, and I tried to lead by example. I thought that if I gently fostered a caring attitude, maybe they would get the point and stop stabbing one another in the back.

My first opportunity as a nurturing role model came as a result of Steve Davis's eyes.

Steve didn't want to be seen as another one of those "jerks from Manhattan," and he worked diligently at diffusing the macho atmosphere of that Chicago office. He believed it was his responsibility to set a new tone by being universally kind and considerate. And he was, most of the time. But every so often, he would come to work in a crabby mood, and since this was out of character for him, no one would be prepared for it, nor could they figure out what they had done to cause his displeasure.

It turned out that they had done nothing. It was the weather. One of Steve's best features was his beautiful *light* blue eyes, and we thought they were what did him in. We all assumed that Steve suffered from seasonal affective disorder (SAD), a common condition for people with light eyes, and when the sun didn't shine for too many days in a row, he would go into a funk that no one could account for, not even Steve.

I started to monitor his bad moods. Sure enough, after two or three days of cloudy weather, Steve would get upset over something petty. So I went on the Internet and ordered lights that duplicate the positive effects of the sun. The day they arrived, we changed all the lighting in his office while he was out for lunch. Everything in Steve's office now had a slightly bluish tint to it. Even Steve. When he found out what we had done, he thought it was funny. But he never removed the lighting, and we don't recall that he ever suffered from SAD again. After that, when he lost his cool, he usually had a good reason, and people knew what that reason was.

The SAD incident gave rise to an expression they used in the office every time something went wrong: "Mama fix." And I was a mother figure in many ways. I tried to correct damaging and unproductive situations with as much care as possible, and the more harsh a correction needed to be, the gentler I was in executing it. For instance, I was very considerate in firing people. I think it's wrong to terminate someone's employment with just the paltry severance that most companies provide, especially when there are families and children involved. I know it's a business circle of life, but it's still painful for me. So to help these people—and to assuage my own conscience—I would always give them advance warning. I'd tell them privately and confidentially that in three months (or four or six) they would be off the payroll. Then I'd stop giving them assignments so that they could use their warning time to find another job. I did this until I weeded out the unproductive people, and then I was very careful in hiring so I wouldn't have to terminate employment for performance reasons again.

Being in touch with this softer side of my personality had other side effects. I nurtured the wounded and gave them confidence. I was collaborative and asked people for their opinions in making decisions, something they weren't accustomed to. And I listened to people without interrupting them. This was hard, though, waiting for them to finish *their* thoughts when really I just wanted to blurt out my own. But I learned to be patient in Chicago.

For the first time I saw that my female side could be as power- ful as the male side I had developed so well at McCann. But had it become too powerful? Was I too collaborative, too nurturing, too understanding, too . . . good? Teamwork is essential, but every team needs a leader whose authority should never be in question. This is *especially* true if you are a woman leading a bunch of rowdy boys. You will be faced with issues a man never has to worry about, and too much TLC can diminish your authority. People may get the impression that you are too nice to be strong. If you get even the slightest inclination that this is happening, nip it in the bud and do it publicly. Sacrifice one or two so that you can save the herd. This happened to me during my second year in Chicago, and it was a painful lesson that had to be learned by everyone.

In trying to overcome my typical New York behavior, I may have overcompensated by being too kind and considerate. Some people began taking advantage of me, and I needed to set the record straight. Everyone needed to know that "Mom" had a little "Dad" in her. I had to bring my male side back and make it clear that I was in control of my creative department. That opportunity came when one of the young men in my creative department overtly disregarded my direction.

Tenney Fairchild was one of my favorites. He was young, talented, and difficult. He had a classic passive-aggressive personality, meaning he wouldn't argue if he disagreed with you; he would just silently dig in his heels and do what he damn well pleased. He was unlike the more up-front Bad Boys on 27, who were always obvious in their rebellion against my authority.

Even though Tenney was "excessively independent" (read: painfully stubborn), he had talent and needed to grow creatively, so I put him in charge of one of our key accounts, the chain of 7-Eleven convenience stores. At this time, 7-Eleven had a bad reputation, and its management had committed millions of dollars to cleaning up its stores and the brand's damaged image. Now we had to tell consumers that 7-Eleven stores were changing and becoming more modern, with improved inventory, wider aisles, and brighter lighting—that they were *not* the same old depressing stores that people were accustomed to and didn't like very much.

All Tenney absorbed from the two-page strategic briefing document was the word "change." (I recognized this selective listening, because it's what my partner Frank Costantini and I used to do when we were responsible for creating ideas.) So Tenney created campaigns about how good and refreshing change was, and during the last five seconds of a thirty-second TV spot, there'd be a mention that 7-Eleven *stores* were changing with a call-to-action line: "Come in and see for yourself."

The spots were entertaining and only a little oblique, but one spot in particular made little sense. It showed a photographer chasing a butterfly through the woods. The notion of a caterpillar "changing" into a butterfly was somehow pivotal in Tenney's mind for demonstrating that, indeed, change was good. I didn't get it.

"What is the butterfly doing in this spot?" I asked.

"It's a metaphor for change and how natural it is . . . as a force of nature."

"But what does that have to do with 7-Eleven?"

"7-Eleven is changing its stores," Tenney explained patiently.

I told him that I knew the stores were changing. "But why is the photographer chasing the butterfly?"

"The photographer is a metaphor for the consumer."

I waited for a punch line. It didn't come.

"Are you kidding me?" I asked.

"No," he said with what appeared to be genuine innocence.

Tenney and I stared at each other for a while. I tried to figure out if he was pulling a prank. (I was often the target of the boys' jokes, and I had to concentrate really hard to know when I was being punked.) Tenney waited to see who would give in first.

"Tenney, *I don't want that damned butterfly spot to leave the agency.*"

I might have even banged my fist on the table for emphasis.

One month later, the rough edits for the campaign were ready to view. (Rough edits, also called rough cuts, are a preliminary version of a TV commercial, and we use them to get client approval before a spot is actually finished with color correction, music, etc.)

And there it was. That damned butterfly being chased by a photographer. Only now the photographer sported a long, straggly beard and carried an antique box camera on a tripod dating back to the turn of the century. Not only did Tenney show the client an idea I had killed, but he filmed it. Even worse, the rough cut made even less sense than the storyboard and script, because now that it was a commercial, the message had to be delivered in *thirty seconds.*

Everyone knew that Tenney had defied me, and they were waiting to see what their too-nice "Mom" would do about it. I did the only thing I could do: I fired him. It killed me to do it, but no one in the creative department ever openly or even secretly defied me again. After that I became known as "Mom . . . with a strong back-hand."

When Tenney's soft-sell campaign about the benefits of change didn't work, we were behind the eight ball. It was clear that 7-Eleven needed a big, hard-ass campaign that would grab people by their lapels and shake them into seeing 7-Eleven differently. But these were gentle, kind clients, and hard-hitting ads didn't feel warm and friendly enough for them.

In order to convince them that they needed a big gun, we put together a little presentation to illustrate why the brand needed a big, bold idea. We brought home the fact that 7-Eleven was the butt of everyone's jokes by making a tape of all the insults people like Jay Leno and David Letterman had made at the expense of the convenience stores. We showed the tape to our 7-Eleven clients at our next meeting. When the tape ended, the clients were laughing, but they got our point. We had them in our corner. I leaned over to Jeff York—the creative person who had edited the tape—and said, "Wouldn't it be great if these comedians could be converted? Will Jay Leno do a commercial?"

It turned out that he wouldn't, but other comedians would. The campaign that Jeff created was funny and dead-on. Each spot opened with a stand-up comedian who would make a funny and derogatory joke about 7-Eleven on the way into a newly renovated store. Once inside the store, the comedian would notice the improvements, and on the way out he or she would remark, begrudgingly, about how the place had changed. When I sold that campaign to our great clients, Jim Notarnicola and Marva Cathey, I told them that I hoped the campaign would be irrelevant in a year. As the stores improved, sure enough, the jokes about 7-Eleven ceased, and after two years the campaign became unnecessary. We had our converted consumers. We were all very happy about that, even though we hated to see the campaign end.

Tenney Fairchild went on to become director of commercials, and later a film writer, director, and producer. Even though I knew he had to go, I still liked the guy, and soon after he left J. Walter Thompson, I gave him an opportunity that I hoped would jumpstart his new career. When Steve Romanenghi and Matt Canzano created the famous "Brain Freeze" spot for the 7-Eleven Slurpee—an idea that was so brilliantly simple, they sold it to me in the hallway and then to our client, Marva Cathey, over the phone—I gave it to Tenney to direct, and he did a great job.

But the "Brain Freeze" spot had another side benefit: I'd made the spot famous, even without much of a media budget, and that helped me win points and loyalty within my creative department. That's really what creative people want the most in life: to be rich and famous, but mostly famous. We were scheduled to run "Brain Freeze" only on MTV, but I knew that it could be a famous spot if we could get a showcase placement, i.e., airtime during a big, important media event with a lot of viewers, such as the Super Bowl, the Academy Awards, or the Grammy Awards. It would be expensive, but it would be worth the price.

I called our media department and said we wanted to run "Brain Freeze" on David Letterman's very first "Late Show" on CBS after leaving his slot on NBC—an event we knew would draw a big audience. They said we could do it and still stay within our media budget. The client approved the decision and the spot aired. Letterman loved the commercial so much the term "Brain Freeze" appeared on his Top 10 list the next night, and he planted Soupy Sales in the audience slurping a Slurpee. We were ecstatic: we had gotten a second "commercial" for Slurpee on Letterman's show for *free*! A couple of weeks later, *USA Today* listed it as the most popular spot on TV that month. It had only run once on CBS and a few times on MTV.

After that, the Bad Boys on 27 started to genuflect when they passed my office. They thought they were being funny, but I loved it. It gave me instant respect and reduced the resentment people had had after I'd fired Tenney.

As my second year at JWT progressed, so did our momentum. We had won back some critical Kraft business, we were in really good shape with our other clients, and we were winning *new* business. The most dazzling triumph was getting into the finals for the coveted $50 million Milk Board review. This was a big piece of business by anyone's standards, and the New York office wanted to do the pitch. Steve Davis and I said no, this one was all ours.

That was a bold move on our parts. If we lost this pitch, Steve and I would be dead meat, mainly because we'd refused help from the New York office. But I had an ace up my sleeve: Tim Kane. Once we had good work, I knew we couldn't lose. In a new-business pitch, more than anything, a prospective client wants to fall in love with an agency. The work and the thinking has to be there, of course, but more than one agency will always have good work. Who will the client fall in love with? That's the important question.

JWT had the best presenter I'd ever seen. When he was "on," Tim Kane could rival the best stand-up comedians, and we won the prestigious $50 million business basically because of his brilliant, funny, and charming presentation of the creative. He had everyone rolling in the aisles: the clients, the consultants, *and* all of us at JWT. We all fell in love. I was never more proud of him.

While I was in Chicago, I always assumed that Tim never heard a word I said to him, but he remembers it differently.

"To your credit, and to my surprise, you never forced me to listen to you," Tim said recently. "Instead of telling me how to fix a script or rewrite a headline, you'd ask, 'So what do you want to do here?' Then you'd give me advice on how to sell it. During the course of this 'chat,' it was always clear what you thought was strongest and what you thought needed to die. But because you didn't force it, we always followed your direction. I know you never believed that, but it's true. At least, there were never any-more Tenney-like insurrections. Now I know, as we all do, that you were just manipulating me so I would do the right thing. But it worked. Kind of."

I had always thought of Tim as my biggest failure. He was al-ready very talented as a writer and presenter, but I knew that he could be a better creative *leader.* I didn't realize until many years later that my nagging had penetrated his thick skull.

"There was a very specific moment when I finally understood what you were trying to do," Tim recalled. "It was during a re-hearsal for the final presentation of the Milk Board pitch. The original plan was that after Steve had done his bit with the Com-modore's* umbrella and Kalasunas† had done his 'mad professor' thing, you and I would stand up and present the creative ideas to-gether. Our pitch consultant said it wasn't working—doing it together was diminishing your stature as the creative director. I fully expected to be relegated to holding the boards. But instead you said, 'Okay, let Tim do it by himself.'

"Now, every agency creative director I'd ever known would've thrown himself in front of a bus before giving up the spotlight. But at that moment, I realized you truly believed that your success would come by making *me* a success. For you, the less formal role would always be the more powerful one. It was a watershed mo-ment for me."

Actually, I made that choice because as good a presenter as I think I am, Tim was better. My ego never trumps my good judg-ment. We won that $50 million Milk Board business, and in three years, we turned the fortunes of JWT/Chicago around. We not only stemmed the decline, we doubled the billings of the office.

---

* The Commodore is JWT's iconic founding-father namesake. We constantly evoked the Commodore's name and image to humanize the agency in new-business pitches.
† Mike Kalasunas was our brilliant and revered director of strategic planning, and he could get away with the most outrageous behavior.

When I left Chicago to return to McCann as chief creative officer, several of the Bad Boys on 27 offered to take me out for a farewell drink. (Not Jägermeister, they were quick to assure me.) I thought it was sweet of them to ask, and that it was probably their way of burying the hatchet. I also assumed that they were so grateful to finally be rid of me, they wanted to celebrate.

So they took me to a bar that served martinis that were famous for including olives stuffed with blue cheese, and before I had my second drink—which they knew would plunge me into oblivion—they said they would all follow me to New York if I wanted them. I was shocked. I thought they were just trying to be nice to a departing boss. But they meant it, those rascals.

I wound up hiring seven of them. Dave Moore was the first. He helped save the AT&T business at McCann and went on to become a brilliant new business player for New York. He was so good that he eventually left me to become the creative director of our Detroit office.

Then I brought in Gib Marquardt, Paul Behnen, Dean Bastian, Tom Jakab, and Hal Walters, a Hasidic Jew who once wrote gags for Jonathan Winters and disarmed everyone with his dry, irreverent wit.

The last one in was the worst of the Bad Boys: Tim Kane himself. All of them have stayed an integral part of my career and my life. They have always been there for me when I needed them with unconditional support and affection.

To this day, there is nothing the Bad Boys on 27 wouldn't do for me. And vice versa.

2

DON'T CLIMB MOUNT EVEREST IN MANOLO BLAHNIKS

Every battle requires weapons. Get some. As women, we have weapons and talents that are uniquely ours, like empathy and intuition, which you have heard about ad nauseam. But if you want to win in the business world, you have to be a player, and that requires skills that you may or may not have already developed. And even if you have these skills, you may believe, like many women, that using them is beneath your dignity.

Get over it.

When you're trying to win with men, use whatever you've got. And whatever you don't already have, you can learn. As my electrical engineer father used to say to me constantly, "Attempt nothing without the proper tools."

The truth is, you are entirely capable of seducing and manipulating your way to the top of boys clubs, if that's where you want to go. At a minimum, you can earn positions of respect and power no matter how far up the ladder you decide to climb. Right now, other people may be making decisions for you, but you can wrest that power away from them and choose what you want yourself. To do this, you need to recognize your innate abilities, acquire whatever skills you don't already have, and use everything with prudence and wisdom. Above all else, be shrewd.

You can start by understanding men.

The bad news is that there are a lot of them in business, and they hold most of the top positions. The good news is that they are not that hard to seduce and manipulate. Most people (including some women) actually enjoy being "handled" as long as you don't hurt them and you operate magnanimously. They won't resent you for manipulating them if you give them something in return, like helping them to be better at their jobs or better people. It's not degrading to operate this way if you know what you are doing, if your heart is in the right place, and if you have the right weapons in your arsenal.

The only caveats about having these weapons are that you must know how to use them and not be afraid to fire a shot.

5

She Cries, She Yells, She Melts, She Squeaks

Everything we've been told about how women are supposed to behave in business is geared to suppress us and make us insecure about ourselves. They tell us don't get angry, don't cry, don't be openly critical—especially to a man—don't be "emotional," don't hope, don't dream, don't ask, don't make *demands*. This advice is . . . how can I put it delicately? *Bullshit!*

Don't believe any of it. Especially the part about not being "emotional." I put this word in quotes because it's so ambiguous. What does it really mean, anyway? When men accuse us of being too "emotional," what are they really talking about? It's either crying or anger that flummoxes them. If we are sensitive, caring, and loving (especially to them), they don't think we are too emotional. It only happens when we lose our temper or composure at *them*. I have asked men why they are so intimidated by us, and they say it's because they don't know how to behave when we cry or lose our cool. It scares them. Of course, they don't have this problem with one another. When a man shows his anger to another man, he is applauded as being strong and uncompromising. If he cries (or weeps, really), it is always for a damn good reason, and that usually has something to do with sports. Either way, he is generally forgiven. Not us. We are penalized. My solution to this is not to do it less. Do it more—but do it judiciously.

It's totally okay for women to show their emotions in business, as long as they know how to use this to their advantage. If it helps you seduce and manipulate, bawl and bellow away. Anger, for example, can be quite effective if you don't overdo it and use it shrewdly. Men will not be afraid or dismissive of women who express their anger in an intelligent, *controlled* fashion. What scares them is hysterics. Anger is permissible, but ranting and raving with no control makes you look like a crazy person. Your reputation and career advancement will be at risk if you are labeled a hothead. Even if you are a "creative" person, fits of temper will only be tolerated so much. Plus, it puts an enormous amount of pressure on you to be talented enough to compensate for being a jerk. I know, because I did all these things at the beginning of my career and learned something from it.

In order to seduce boys clubs, you need to use everything you have at your disposal, including a palette of strong emotions. Men have to know that you are in the room and are a force to be reckoned with. The worst thing that can happen is to be ignored. Work hard and squeak when you feel you need some oil.

As women in business, we have to be able to show our displeasure with people and with circumstances, otherwise we will be little more than Stepford wives. I think the best barometer for when to use anger is to make certain it's not personal. You can tell the difference when you hear yourself saying things like:

"How dare you undermine *me*?"

"He made *me* fail."

"This is bad for *me*."

You can see where these examples are a little self-serving. You'll be on safer ground if you get angry on behalf of the company, in defense of your colleagues, or to protect the quality of your work.

Remember, no one blames the mother bear for guarding her cub, but no one wants to hang out with her either. And if she becomes too enthusiastic with her defense, someone from animal control will come along and put her down. I'm not saying this will happen to you; maybe they'll use a stun gun or something, but be careful, just in case.

An angry outburst on occasion may also be forgiven if you have other qualities that are more nurturing. It's like tough love from your mother. You know she loves you, but once in a while she has to give you an attitude adjustment. In my family, that adjustment came with the meeting of my mother's hand to our behinds, but we still felt loved. Nurture the people you lead and they will put your "attitude adjustments" in the proper perspective.

And one last thing: Always yell up or across, never down. It's unfair to yell at people who have no defense against you.

Meltdowns and Mayhem

I'd like to say that I learned my lesson back in Richmond, when my angry outburst while eating an apple almost killed me. It would be a lie, but I'd like to be able to say it anyway. Learning from one's mistakes is a sign of maturity. Still, I matured slowly and had meltdowns of various sizes and shapes. The last really big one happened right before I left McCann Erickson to become the executive creative director at JWT/Chicago.

I was a group creative director managing the Alka-Seltzer business with a very difficult client, who was the director of Alka-Seltzer's marketing. The man was on a mission: He wanted to revitalize the flagging brand and go down in history as a marketing genius. Who could blame him?

Everyone loved the Alka-Seltzer brand; they just weren't buying the Alka-Seltzer products. They loved the brand because they still remembered the company's famous and award-winning advertising, which started with the little guy himself.

Speedy Alka-Seltzer—one of the most endearing icons in the advertising business—sold the effervescent tablets to relieve heartburn, acid indigestion, upset stomachs, headaches, body aches, and general pain. In other words, too much food and booze. Singing one of the most famous jingles ever written ("Plop, plop, fizz, fizz, oh, what a relief it is"), Speedy sold his little heart out in more than two hundred television commercials from 1953 to 1964.

In 1972, Alka-Seltzer's "I Can't Believe I Ate the Whole Thing" ad ran on TV, and the phrase became one of the ten most memorable lines of the decade, according to *Newsweek* magazine. But the most brilliant Alka-Seltzer commercial of all time was the simplest: It aired in 1969 and featured George Raft, the actor famous for his bad-guy roles in forties film noir movies. It was called "The Unfinished Lunch."

In the spot, George Raft and about a hundred other convicts are in a prison lunchroom. He takes a bite of the terrible prison food and, recoiling in disgust, takes his metal cup and starts banging it slowly and deliberately on the metal lunchroom table while chanting "Alka-Seltzer." Then the convict next to him does the same thing. Then another and another, until the whole room of inmates is banging cups and joining Raft in his chant of "Alka-Seltzer, Alka-Seltzer, Alka-Seltzer." The spot ends on the promise, "For fast relief . . . Alka-Seltzer."

But when I came onboard, there hadn't been a great Alka-Seltzer ad in more than a decade. The client was determined to change that with a $15 million budget—which wasn't a lot of money for a mass-marketed brand that was supposed to appeal to everyone who ate or drank too much. In order for the money to do the job, the advertising would have to work hard to be noticed and remembered (this is called "Recall"), and it would have to be persuasive in getting people to buy the product (this is called "Purchase Intent" or "Persuasion"). I added one more requirement: The advertising would have to measure up to the creative standard of the famous Alka-Seltzer advertising of the past.

The stewards of the brand weren't worried about getting popular ads on the air. They just wanted the work to test well so that they could prove they did their job. As a result, it was very difficult to sell the marketing director anything good, and when he finally agreed to test a creative idea, his expectations were unrealistic. This put an enormous pressure on me to produce and air something that would test well and not publicly humiliate me. (Public Humiliation is still the best motivator for all creative people.)

There were two key people who ran the Alka-Seltzer business with me: one was my art director/creative director partner and good friend, Steve Ohler. Steve was a Kevin Costner look-alike who was then and still is one of the most decent men on the planet. The other was Rob McKinley, the most senior account manager on the business, who looked like a disheveled Robert Redford. The three of us were perfectly matched, because Steve and I were passionate worriers while Rob was just the opposite. He never appeared to worry about anything. In fact, he never even wore a watch, which used to drive me crazy.

"How can you not wear a watch?"

"I've never worn one." He was always answering my questions with non sequiturs. It was his way of avoiding an issue.

"How do you know what time it is?"

"I always know what time it is."

"What time is it now?"

"Ten-thirty."

And he'd be right. It would be ten-thirty.

"How did you know?"

"I looked at your watch."

"Aren't you afraid you'll be late for meetings?"

"Am I ever late?"

We had this *Groundhog Day*–like exchange regularly. To this day, Rob doesn't own a watch. Why are aggravating men so often the most interesting?

As frustrating as Rob could be at times, he always made Steve and me laugh, and it was this camaraderie that got us through our "Year of the Alka-Seltzer." Our meetings were excruciatingly painful, and the three of us were worn out from servicing the account.

Alka-Seltzer's headquarters were in Elkhart, Indiana, and just the mere effort of traveling there was physically as well as psychologically painful. We would leave our homes at 5:30 in the morning, catch the 7 A.M. flight to Chicago, and then hop on a puddle-jumper to Elkhart. We would arrive at the meetings by 11:30 A.M., watch the clients eat lunch in front of us without ever offering us something to eat (I swear), show them three or four campaigns, hear the work was all off-strategy because they had changed the strategy the day before without consulting us, and then trudge back home the same way we came to collapse in our beds by midnight.

The only fun we had was with one another, and on the flights back we would find something about the meeting to laugh at. Actually, the worse the meeting was, the more we would laugh. It might have been a form of hysteria, come to think of it.

We went through this Alka-Seltzer routine twice a month. In between meetings, Steve and I struggled to develop work that would get approved and ultimately tested, so we could get something on the air. While Steve and I were the main team on Alka-Seltzer, we were also the creative team on Ritz crackers, and we wrote and produced spots for a Ritz campaign that tested really well. We also supervised other businesses in my group: Steve handled Waterman Pens, and I ran our biggest account, AT&T. We were always exhausted, and anyone who saw us during this period knew that the only thing keeping us going were a fear of failure and huge amounts of adrenaline.

After a year of this physical and emotional punishment, McCann got a new general manager for the New York office, and one of his first inspirations was to lend us a hand on Alka-Seltzer. He immediately earned the nickname "Skippy" because he was so gosh-darned gung *ho*. He also had a habit of explaining things to me while he drew square boxes on a yellow pad. All of his ideas were printed neatly *inside* the boxes. Frankly, he scared me.

One day, Skippy had an idea for Alka-Seltzer that he was sure would save our hides, and he couldn't wait to share it with me. I begged Rob to make Skippy go away, but instead he tells our new boss that I was having a nervous breakdown and couldn't see anyone. Skippy tells Rob to get me under control, or else he will do it himself. Rob encourages him to try, assuring him that I would listen to a higher authority.

It was a mean thing for Rob to do, and Skippy was totally unprepared for what happened next. The two men came to see me for a chat. Rob could barely disguise his glee as he followed Skippy into my office. But Skippy was so intent on his mission, he didn't read the room. First of all, my office stank of cigarette smoke because I'd been chain-smoking. Second, the place looked like a bomb site, littered with storyboards, empty Diet Coke cans, and half-eaten sandwiches. And third, my eyes were red and bleary because Steve and I had been working late every night and not sleeping. But the biggest clue was on my wall. It was a huge sign that said:

Alka-Seltzer Escape Kit

Mounted under the sign were two safety razor blades labeled "His" and "Hers." When Skippy and Rob came in unannounced, Steve was sitting on my sofa with his head in his hands and I was pacing, kicking a path through the mountains of crap on the floor. Skippy immediately announced that he had an idea.

His idea is that we put an actor in a tight close-up in front of a locked camera (meaning it would have no movement). The actor holds up a box of Alka-Seltzer in one hand and tells us that this product is ideal for two, two, two—and the actor should hold up two fingers really close to his face, because the camera is tightly framed on him—two remedies in one. For headache *and* upset stomach. This is the strategy, after all, and we should be very simple and clear with the communication. No jokes or anything extraneous (like a creative *idea*) to distract the viewer from the "message."

Skippy decides that because I appear dumbstruck it means I didn't understand his commercial. So he acts it out again. This time he holds up a pack of my cigarettes to represent the box of Alka-Seltzer and smashes it against his cheek. He holds up two fingers next to his other cheek to once again demonstrate the "action" in the commercial.

"Is it for headaches? Or upset stomachs? Why, it's for *both*," Skippy says, smiling broadly. Then he winks at me. I think it was the wink that set me off, but I still didn't say anything. What could I say? Now Skippy thinks my silence is due to the very real possibility that I just might be a moron after all.

"Get it?" he finally asks me.

I look at Rob, who stares back at me, his blue eyes round with wonder and delight. He is struggling with every ounce of his being not to laugh and he keeps coughing to mask his loss of control.

"Get it?" Skippy asks me again.

I grab the "Hers" razor blade from our Alka-Seltzer Escape Kit and slam it on my desk. Then I hold out my wrists to Skippy.

"Go ahead. Slit my wrist now. Might as well slit *both* of them, because the only *freaking* way in freaking *hell* that this agency will do an Alka-*freaking*-Seltzer commercial with a talking head saying 'two, two, two mints in one'* is *over my fucking dead body*. I will be a pariah in this business. I will go down in history as the *hack* who single-handedly *destroyed* the Alka-Seltzer brand. I would rather die, and I'll take *you* with me. AAAAUUUUUGGGGGHHHHH! Get OUT!"

Skippy's face goes ashen. He throws the pack of cigarettes on my desk and tells me I smoke too much. As he follows Rob out of my office, I slam the door really hard, trying to hit his butt on his way out. Someone in the hall hears his exit conversation.

"Is she always like this?" Skippy asks Rob.

To which my good friend Mr. McKinley replies:

"Pretty much."

After that incident, Skippy always talked to me as if I were a lunatic: slowly, deliberately, and very calmly, as if anything he said could spook me and set me off on another hysterical tantrum. It was amusing for a while until it became annoying. At least he never tried to dictate a creative solution to me again.

I never got better at handling that Alka-Seltzer client, and the business never improved while I was calling the shots. Sean Fitzpatrick, the new creative director at McCann New York, tried to help. When he heard about how we were being treated, he sent a note to the Alka-Seltzer client that said, "Feed my people." They did. But they still didn't buy any work from us.

Finally, Sean found the perfect motivation for me.

"Fix it," he said. "If we lose the business, I'll make you fire four people."

It was the only thing he could say to make me admit defeat and relinquish control of that business. But I learned a lesson: Trying to do everything yourself can be detrimental (as well as unnecessary), and a confident person knows when to defer to someone

---

* "Two, Two, Two Mints in One" was Certs's positioning for years. It answered the important question: "Is it a breath mint or a candy mint?"

who can do a better job. Delegating is a hard concept for a controlling person to embrace. It takes courage to allow others to do a job you believe you can do better, and even more strength of character to live with their solutions. But I had no choice. I gave the business to one of my associate creative directors, who wrote a jingle with vignettes showing people going about their busy daily lives, not allowing headaches or upset stomachs to slow them down. The client bought it. My associate creative director was a hero, and I allowed him to run the business with autonomy. His campaign ran for two years, and Alka-Seltzer's sales improved. Even a jingle with vignettes was better than running nothing at all.

About six months later I left for JWT/Chicago to run its creative department, and for three years there I rarely lost my temper. But even before that move to the overly sensitive Midwest, I knew that shouting did not require any great skill. Any idiot can yell. I just believed that the easiest way for me to manipulate people, especially men, was with a short fuse. I thought that if they were afraid of my temper, they would tread more softly around me. It would take me a long time to get that *totally* out of my system.

And yet, I did learn something about controlling meltdowns along the way. For instance, now I count to ten before I react to even the most imbecilic behavior. If someone makes a horrible suggestion that will ruin my life, I calmly count to ten in my head so that it will appear that I am actually thinking about the merits of the idea. Then I say, "Okay, that sounds good to me. Let me take a crack at it." When I come back and say the suggestion didn't work, it will appear as though I sincerely tried it and it truly didn't work. It's better than dying of asphyxiation (from an apple) or bleeding to death (from a razor blade).

Another lesson I learned was to choose my audience with care. It's never a great idea to have a meltdown in front of your boss, and especially not in front of an audience, even if you know unequivocally that you are right and someone else is wrong. If I had stayed at McCann, I would not have had a fan in Skippy. It was fortunate for me that I left for Chicago soon after my meltdown with him.

And the last lesson I learned was, when someone makes you crazy, take Alka-Seltzer for fast relief from a pain in the head *and* a pain in the ass. Two, two, two remedies in one!

Is There Crying in Advertising?

If there's a place for anger in your repertoire of emotions, then what about tears? We're told not to cry in the office because it makes us look weak. But is that entirely true? Can tears be useful in seducing and manipulating men in the office? It depends on why we are leaking water. If we're crying because we're hurt (and they hurt us) or because we're also angry (a double whammy), it makes them very uncomfortable. But men don't object if we weep. Weeping is what they call their own tears. They don't *cry*—unless they have a good reason to bawl, like the men at McCann when the Yankees lose to the Boston Red Sox. *Then* there is crying in baseball.

I've shed tears in the office more than once. Sometimes it paid off and other times it didn't. This is a slippery slope (as we like to say in advertising), because you don't want to be seen as a wimp or a weakling, and yet it always gets a man's attention. If you are a strong person by nature, a wobbly voice and tear on occasion can soften even the toughest man. For instance, the strongest alpha male I know is my long-term partner and current COO of McCann Worldgroup, Eric Keshin, and the few times I blubbered with him, I brought him to his knees. He hates to see me defeated enough to lose my composure and always comes to my defense on those oc-casions. The time it didn't pay off was when I blubbered in front of my boss, John Nieman, but that had more to do with him than it did with me.

John was my group creative director at Y&R, and I was one of his associate creative directors. Back then I always felt over-whelmed, because I was managing too many businesses: Kentucky Fried Chicken, Thomas' English Muffins, *Time* and *People* magazines. They were all good but time-consuming clients. And in my opinion, I never had enough people helping me.

John had an interesting management style, especially with me. I would go into his office and complain that I needed more creative people—only he never had more people to give me. All he had was smoke and mirrors. So he would direct me to a piece of furniture in his office that had once been a file cabinet in a library. It had about five hundred little drawers, and each drawer held one of John's magic tricks. He was an amateur magician and quite excellent at it, but what made him great wasn't so much the tricks as the funny patter he used while performing them. Since I'm a sucker for sleight of hand, he was always able to snap me out of my doldrums with a few good tricks. He also knew that I had a short attention span and magic was an easy way to distract me when I came to see him about a problem.

On this particular day I was in a panic because I had to be in three places at the same time. I barged into his office and explained my predicament to him. I started my explanation calmly enough.

"I have to cover the radio production for Thomas' English Muffins because the writer . . . *my* writer . . . is *on a shoot for some-one else's business;* I have a preproduction meeting for the most complicated KFC spot ever created because I *am* the writer on that one; and I have *the client from hell* (from *Time* magazine) waiting in my office so she can find one more *frigging* way to *FRIGGING* humiliate me creatively with one more print ad that doesn't make sense and has to be released in *TWO FUCKING HOURS.*"

By this time I had lost all rational thought. I couldn't even remember to say "frigging" instead of the crude, but effective, "fucking," and I didn't even care.

"What am I going to do?" I complain. *"What am I going to DO?* I need more help, John. I can't operate this way. I can't be in three places at the same time. *Oh God, I'm going to die."*

Nieman looked at me with a calm, blank expression, which only served to piss me off more, and said, "Go open a drawer."

"I don't need a magic trick, John. I need a miracle."

He looks hurt, and now I'm thinking that I have hurt *his* feelings. *I have hurt him.* How does he turn the tables on me like this? In addition to being hysterical, now *I FEEL GUILTY.* I start to cry, and in order to mask how pathetic it is to cry in front of my boss, I layer on anger, hoping that fury will trump the weakness of tears. It was a complicated maneuver, and I did *not* master it.

So now I am crying *and* yelling and I'm sure he's going to kick me out of his office. But instead, he quietly gives me the best advice I ever got. He tells me that I will always be juggling too many things, it's in my nature, and something is always going to fall through the cracks. The only question is, who will decide what takes the fall? He then strongly suggests that I be the one to make that call instead of having circumstance make it for me.

"At least you will have the illusion of being in control," he says.

That was the only real magic I was going to get from him.

So first I met with the *Time* client, and instead of having our usual protracted "chat" about which photograph looked better in an ad, I just told her she could use whichever photo she wanted. Meetings with this controlling woman always took less time when the burden of creativity was removed. Both photographs were good anyway (only my selection was slightly better). In the long run, no one gave a damn. That meeting lasted five minutes.

Then I dashed over to the preproduction meeting for the KFC television shoot (also a client meeting), and I let one of the agency producers handle the radio production for Thomas' English Muffins. I hated the finished spot and had to re-record it the next day. That cost $1,250 in talent and studio costs, which the agency ate. No one gave a damn about that, either.

Deciding which ball I am going to drop is a "Sophie's choice" for me, because I always think everything is equally critical. It still upsets me to have to make these kinds of choices, but I don't cry about them anymore. As I grew up and matured as a leader, I began crying about more important things.

The best crying story I have is now part of McCann Erickson lore. It is *alleged* that I shed tears in a client meeting, and while this is accurate, it is not precisely true. There was no real moisture involved, but there *was* a lot of emotion, and there was definitely the *suggestion* that my eyes would spring a leak.

The incident happened during a presentation for the $700 million Verizon Wireless business. It was an odd pitch to begin with, because we already had an ongoing relationship with John Stratton, the chief marketing officer of the company. Most of the time, new business prospects are strangers. John is tough but fair and has a "take the hill" mentality that is inflexible. He looks for the same traits in the people and the companies he does business with. It was why McCann's take-no-prisoners, alpha-male persona was appealing to him. We were made for each other.

We had been slaving away for Stratton for almost half a year on a trial basis, creating and producing all of his day-to-day assignments to show him we could handle the enormous amount of work his business generated. At the same time, we were pitching him new ideas to show him that we were big thinkers and the kind of agency that he could be proud to call his own for the long term.

At one meeting, toward the end of his six-month decision-making process, we had just given him a big idea to encourage consumer loyalty ("Get in"). There was a lull in the meeting, and since I was tired, I mumbled something with a whine.

"So, John, are we getting married here or what? It only took my husband *two* months of dating to pop the question to *me*."

It was so unexpected that Stratton burst out laughing. I'd like to say he was also so disarmed that he awarded us the business on the spot, but we didn't get it for another month. Our final pitch for the Verizon Wireless business would be the scene of what Eric Keshin likes to call my "crying jag," but it didn't exactly happen that way.

Our final presentation was to John Stratton and two critical men in his organization: the chief operating officer and the CEO, who ran the entire Verizon Wireless dynasty.

Part of our assignment was to introduce V CAST, a new technology that made a phone the center for entertainment with sophisticated downloads and broadcast content, which included programming designed just for mobile phones. This technology is now advancing with lightning speed, but at the time it was so new, even the most senior clients had seen only a prototype; they had never actually held a working V CAST phone in their hands.

Our strategy for winning this business was to prove that we were the ninja agency they coveted, so we sent Suresh Nair, McCann's codirector of strategic planning, to Korea, where the technology was already a few years old. For Suresh it was like taking a trip in a time machine and fast-forwarding five years into the future. The Koreans were so far ahead of us that they were able to download movies on their phones. As they would watch one fifteen-minute segment of a movie, it would be replaced with the next fifteen-minute segment. It was awesome. Suresh not only bought a phone and downloaded a hot Britney Spears music video, he hired a film crew and taped himself on the streets of Seoul showing people the video with Britney seducing some guy in an airplane bathroom all on his amazing V CAST phone.

Our clients were blown away, not just with the Britney Spears video, which they watched three times, but also with the fact that we flew to Korea to get firsthand experience with this new technology. I knew we had the business even before we showed them our brilliant creative ideas that would knock their socks off. But Eric Keshin had some last words of encouragement for me just minutes before the meeting started. "I don't care how confident you think you are when this meeting is over," he whispered in my ear. "Ask for the frigging business."

So I made this close:

"For the last six months, we have made *several* presentations for your business, as if we weren't already working with you, as if we had not produced thirty television commercials and two hundred print ads, not to mention the five TV spots we have in production at this very moment.

"We didn't rest on our laurels or assume that any ongoing relationship with Verizon Wireless would give us an advantage. In fact, if anything, we were probably at a disadvantage, because we knew some of you wanted a clean slate.

"But now that this lengthy process is over, I have to say this: There is no reason to take this business away from us. We have learned a lot in a short time. We know that our job for you is never done, that battles have to be won every day, and that nothing can be taken for granted. We have lived this philosophy, and we have what it takes to continue living it as a way of life.

"You cannot replicate in any new-business pitch what it takes to do this job successfully for you. And believe me, yours is not a business for the faint of heart. But we have managed it now for almost six months. We have a shorthand with the people in this room, we believe in you, we trust you, we want you to succeed, and we think you know that about us.

"And we have never failed you. We have never failed to deliver for you quickly and with exceptional creative work. We have never failed to give you one hundred and fifty percent of our time, emotions, and brainpower.

"There is a bond between McCann Erickson and Verizon Wireless. We belong together. . . ."

At this point, I admit, a little emotion had crept into my quivering voice. In fairness, it did appear as though tears would be springing from my eyes at any moment, but I pressed on to my close.

"We don't want you to take this business away from us. We don't *deserve* to lose it." I paused for a second and then said, "I'm supposed to ask if you have any questions now. Do you?"

John Stratton was staring at me, willing me with all his might to keep it together and not cry in front of his COO and CEO. Meanwhile, the chief operating officer, who also thought I was about to embarrass myself, winked at me and gave me an encouraging little smile. The CEO just glared at all of us. Later I found out that we had blown him away, and he realized that there was no way he could even consider other agencies. And as time went by, he became more and more pleased with that decision.

Everyone went back to McCann, and within minutes it was all over the agency that I had cried for the business at the Verizon Wireless pitch. Believe me, if that's what it would have taken to keep that huge piece of business, I would have bawled like a baby, but I used other emotions that were even better than tears. During that two-minute close, I totally dropped my defenses and was completely honest and vulnerable in front of them, even while I was making a well-thought-out and reasoned argument as to why they should give us their business. As the creative director and emotional leader of the McCann team, I was able to show how personally invested we all were in them and their business.

Later the next day, when we were officially awarded the entire account of $700 million in billings (a business that is still growing for us), our CEO, John Dooner, told me how important that win was. If we hadn't gotten it, not only would Interpublic Group (our holding company) have lost all that revenue for McCann, but there was an additional $20 million in *revenue* (not billings) that would have been lost at other IPG companies, which also had large pieces of the Verizon Wireless business.

"I didn't want to put any additional pressure on you before-hand," Dooner said, grinning at me. "I didn't want you to start bawling at the *beginning* of the meeting, too."

Strangely enough, I was a hero for almost losing it at that meeting, and people still talk about it. But there was one big difference in that emotional display: It showed passion and commitment. Not fear, anger, or frustration.

And only a woman could have pulled it off. No doubt about it.

––––––

Oh, and one more thing: Two years later, John Stratton was promoted to chief marketing officer for the entire Verizon business, and six months after that, he gave McCann the rest of his business. More than $1.2 billion in total spending.

No one cried at that meeting.

6

It's Hard to Seduce Strangers

In any kind of interaction, whether it's adversarial or amorous, it's essential to know your quarry. It's very difficult and time-consuming to seduce someone when you don't know his sweet spots. If you hope to succeed in a boys club, you absolutely must understand the men you are trying to influence and eventually control. Whether you want them to follow you off a cliff or just protect you from danger, you must uncover what makes each of them tick. You can label this process anything you want: manipulation, maneuvering, invisible persuasion. Whatever. Just get under their skin. Find their buttons and push them.

Maggie was a smart woman who worked with male colleagues who always excluded her. The men would hang out with one another and make business decisions while they were out drinking, having lunch, or playing pool. Maggie never knew what was going on. She could have whined and complained that they were not being team players. She could have threatened them or had tantrums, but that would only have made them exclude her even more. Instead, she figured out a way to seduce them and manipulate their behavior. What do men love, Maggie asked herself? Beer. Candy. Toys. So she stocked her mini-fridge with beer, along with her designer water; she kept a big bowl of candy on her desk; and she brought in games like Boggle and checkers. Pretty soon the boys were hanging out in *her* office, and when they discussed things of business interest, Maggie was right there with them, listening and participating.

Here's another obvious observation: We all admire people who remind us of ourselves. And yet most women don't understand this when they are sparring with men. That charming rogue Henry Higgins hit it right on the head when, baffled by the indomitable Eliza Doolittle, he asked the question most men ask themselves all the time: "Why can't a woman be more like a man?" Well, we can. In fact, we *must* be more like them if we want to compete with them.

If men don't feel comfortable with us, they will not allow us to play with them. We can't change their behavior, but we can change ours. In becoming more like them, we not only make them more comfortable with us, but we actually learn some of their admirable male skills that lead to success. Like their random acts of bravery, their ability to laugh and have fun, their eagerness to take credit for what they do, and their ability to stand up for themselves. They are also much more constant than we are, much more predictable. Men are not baffling—at least, not to one another. They don't send out mixed signals like we do.

"Open the door."

"Don't open the door."

"I'm not having sex with you because you bought dinner." Then, when he doesn't make a pass on the first date: *"I know. You're just not 'into' me, right?"*

We tell men how to behave, but we're not consistent with our directions:

"Be strong."

"Be sensitive."

"Be masterful."

"Don't boss me around."

"Be there when I need you."

"Don't solve my problems for me."

What do we *want* from them? They're confused. We're an enigma to them, and men are afraid of the unknown. And when they're scared, they are not confident or comfortable. We don't need to eliminate stirring up their basic apprehension altogether. Sometimes a little mystery can work to our advantage, but we do need to understand our capricious behavior and manage it.

For instance, it's pointless to mystify men at work. Be honest about what you want from them. Tell them when you need their help, and especially when you don't. Sometimes they think they are protecting us, but aren't they really just holding us back? I don't like it when men treat women like fragile little flowers. It's okay to be vulnerable with them, because sometimes we need their strength, but not at the cost of our independence and self-reliance. If that's the price we have to pay for them to "hold the door," we'll hold our own bloody doors. I'm also wary when they put us on a pedestal. They think they are doing us a favor, but you can't get your uniform dirty if you're high up in the air. You need to be on the ground for that. You need to be in the thick of it.

It's important to be very clear and straightforward with men. If you want to be a player, you have to act like one and accept the consequences. Sooner or later, if you are an *asset* to them, they will let you join their club.

And that's another thing.

What do men love more than sex?

Money.

Learn this lesson early and don't forget it. If you are a rainmaker and you bring in the money, men will love you. You won't even have to follow *any* rules. Not the time-honored ones, or even the new ones that challenge tradition. You won't even have to seduce and manipulate all that much. Money is the great equalizer. The ability to make money in a boys club is the fastest way to become a member, and if you make enough money, they will even follow your lead.

Another way to become a member is to drink their Kool-Aid. Wrap your head around their annoying little foibles and try to find them endearing.

My husband and I have GPS navigation systems in our cars, and a female voice gives directions. Brian is always at odds with this poor woman, since he prides himself on his flawless sense of direction and she is in flagrant competition with him. His irritation with her is totally alien to his true character.

"Can you *believe* where she is taking me? Christ."

"She doesn't know *what* she is talking about."

"I'm not following *her*. We'll wind up in Detroit on this road."

I solve the problem by turning our navigation system off.

While women are usually open to improvement, men view suggestions as criticism. If I say to a female creative person, "Your idea is off-strategy," she will do one of two things. She'll either examine the strategy to prove her interpretation is correct, or she will go back to her office and make sure her idea executes the strategy. If I make the same comment to a man, he will dismiss my critique and say, "The *strategy* is wrong."

The assumption that men don't listen at all is a mistake. You must accept this. They do listen; it's just that their brains process what their minds *want* to hear, and this makes them even more slippery. When you say to a man, "This might be good on Mars, but on Earth and in my creative department and on this piece of business, it just won't fly," all he has heard is, "*This is good.*" A man listens selectively—just like a dog, and I mean that with all due affection. I love dogs. They are just more high-maintenance than

cats. Once I understood these dynamics, I was much better at con-
vincing men to take my direction at work.

Unquestionably, the women I work with give me far less aggravation than the men. I use a mental shorthand with the women;
we understand one another. They can read my face and body language (no matter how subtle), and they listen to what I'm *actually*
saying, not what they think I *should* be saying. That doesn't mean
that they don't fight for what they believe in, they just know the
difference between a "no" that is uncontestable and a "no" that is
negotiable. With men, everything is negotiable, especially with a
female boss.

Here's the difference between two teams presenting creative
work to me. It is a level playing field. All four of these people know
me very well. They know the clients and have worked on the
client's business before. Both teams are presenting clever but inappropriate humor.

Two men present an idea: Bob and Dennis are a clever and productive team, and they are responsible for some of the smartest,
edgiest work in the agency. Bob is a Brit. He knows he is good, and
he is a bit arrogant. I say "a bit" because I really like him, and I am
constantly making allowances for his difficult behavior. He is a
very funny and intelligent royal pain in the ass. Dennis is equally
creative, but he is quietly confident. The two men come into my
office to show me a television campaign they have just conceived.

First, they play with everything that is lying around on my conference table: toy cap guns, a Rubik's Cube, a bowl filled with
candy. Then they flirt with me, trying to decide if I am in a good
mood or not.

"You look so refreshed," Bob the Brit will say.

"Did you have a face-lift over the weekend?" Dennis asks.

"Easy, lad," the Brit says. "She doesn't need a face-lift; she has
youth written all over her face."

They are trying to butter me up so I will buy their work. I have unintentionally taught them this kind of manipulation, only they are much more heavy-handed and obvious than I am when I do it to them.

They present their idea well and with enthusiasm, acting out all the parts and doing a bang-up job. Normally, when they show me something good, they get big smiles, but this time they are mostly getting frowns. Then I make one fatal mistake: I can't help myself, and a laugh bursts its way out of my mouth. It *is* funny work, even though it is totally inappropriate for the client and assignment. I shouldn't have laughed. Laughter trumps a frown. All they have retained now is that their work is funny.

"Don't you love it?" This is a rhetorical question. They assume that I do.

"Hmm. Did you try anything else?" I ask them.

"No. This was our best idea. Don't you love it?"

Now I have a pained expression on my face. I realize that subtlety will be lost on them.

"It's hysterical, right?" they say, grinning at me.

Here's my problem. It *is* funny and very imaginative, but it's still wrong. The client will crucify me if I let this go through. I have to decide which disastrous meeting I want to have: the one with the client or the one with this team.

"It's funny," I say, and they beam at me, "but it's not right for this client. *This* client doesn't like broad jokes. They like heartwarming, charming humor. Fun, maybe, but not fun*ny*."

They still only hear "It's funny."

"Yeah, we love it, too. Can you sell it to them?" (They mean the client.) They are already producing the spots in their heads and thinking about directors. They are not listening to me.

I try a different tactic.

"I know you love it," I say, "but it's not right. Remember the campaign you did for these guys last year? You loved that, too, but we couldn't sell it. In fact, they got mad at you, and you went back to the well and did something else, something so much better . . . *so* much better. And now they love you. They trust you."

"So what are you saying?" They are starting to get uneasy.

"I'm saying that this won't fly. It's not right, it's inappropriate for the brand, and truth be told"—I'm whispering now—"it's actually off-strategy. It can't be the only campaign we show them. Do something else, because these clients, who at the moment think we are very smart, will think we have *lost our freaking minds.*"

"So you're not going to even *try* to sell it?" Their lips are curling into either a snarl or a whimper. I can't tell; a snarl, probably.

At this point I would rather eat dirt than present their creative to this client, but instead I say *gently* and with whatever sympathy I can dredge up, because now I'm getting tired, "It would be a mistake."

They explode. "That's the trouble with this agency. *No one* stands behind breakthrough work. This place *sucks.* The client *sucks.*"

What they mean is that *I* suck, but they have miraculously tapped into a vein of judgment buried deep inside their brains and they realize they have already pushed me far enough. If they weren't really good creative people, if they didn't always come through for me, if they didn't always pull a miracle out of a hat, if I didn't have a lot of affection for them under normal circumstances, I would shoot them now. But instead I reach for my last resort: child psychology.

"That's exactly what you said last time," I tell them, "and then you did something better, something brilliant, something they bought that you produced and put on your reel. Why can't you do something like that again? Something that is fun and charming and *appropriate for the brand*?"

"So what are you *saying*?"

I pick up my metaphorical two-by-four and bop them on their heads.

"What I'm saying is that you need to leave my office in a huge huff, go back to your own offices, slam your doors, curse me for the gutless wonder that I am, and then do something else. This isn't going anywhere. It's certainly not leaving the agency. Oh, and don't just fish something out of your wastebaskets. It has to be *good* as well as appropriate."

The result: Presenting the work, 10 minutes. Killing it, 30 minutes.

Bob and Dennis leave in a huff, and I hear a door slam down the hall. Two days later they come back with a brilliant campaign that even *they* realize is better than their first "breakthrough" idea. But I renege and let them present both campaigns to the client, because I have to let them find out for themselves that I was right. The clients laugh at the first campaign but buy the second one, and they fall all over Bob and Dennis, lavishing them with praise and admiration. They are heroes. They go off to Rio to shoot for two weeks.

Okay, now two women present an idea: Linda and Lulu have been at the agency for several years, and they have a reputation as home-run hitters. They are the go-to team whenever we need a clever, big idea quickly, and they rarely strike out. The two women come into my office to show me their creative work. We spend a few minutes talking about important things like hair, makeup, relationships, and the eternal appeal of George Clooney. Then they present their idea, and are charming and funny. I laugh with them and smile, but when they are finished, I have a slight frown.

"You hate it," they say immediately.

"I don't hate it," I say. "It's hysterical, but it's just not appropriate for the brand. The humor is brilliant, but it's too broad and it's way off-strategy."

They are disappointed. "Okay. You don't think we could tone it down?"

I feel sorry for them. They really like their work, but I have to be honest: "If you tone it down, you lose what's fun about it. And it would still be off-strategy."

They look dejected. I tell them not to be defeated, that the idea was great, really wonderful, and that they are a smart, funny team. I assure them that they will do something else even better. Without a doubt.

They think about it for a while and say, "Okay. We'll be back."

As the art director leaves, I say encouragingly, "*Love* your shoes."

They leave crushed, but they are already talking about something else they could try.

The result: Presenting the work, 10 minutes. Killing it, 5 minutes.

In two days the women come back with a campaign that is dead-on. The client, self-diagnosed as "difficult," falls all over them with praise and admiration. They are heroes. They go off to Vienna to shoot for two weeks.

Weapons That Disarm

One of the great tools, or weapons, we have as women is flirting, and men always respond well to positive attention. If you know you are going to have a contentious meeting with a man, you can defuse his anger before he even opens his mouth. Unless he is morbidly obese, there is no man on earth who won't puff up at this sentence:

"Wow, you look great. Been working out?"

Or, if you "accidentally" touch a man's arm while you are talking about something serious, you can interrupt yourself with a quick show of admiration:

"Wow, your arm is like steel. Been working out?"

I know, I know, it's obvious and underhanded, but it *always* works.

Another way to diffuse and disarm is with unexpected humor, but you really have to know your quarry to pull this off.

Irwin Warren was one of four executive creative directors who reported directly to me as McCann's chief creative officer. Even he would admit that he was high-maintenance. Irwin had asked to meet with me because he was furious about something. He asked for meetings on a regular basis, and neither one of us can remember what this particular infringement on his peace of mind was. Sometimes he just needed to vent.

Irwin poured out his anger and frustration for a solid fifteen minutes over whatever his angst du jour was. I watched him intently while he flailed his arms, ranting and raving. When he finished, I put my hand on his knee and leaned in to him, staring at his wavy, snowy white hair.

"You know," I said, "if you just put a blond rinse in your hair, it would look *great*." He paused for a moment, glaring at me. Then he burst out laughing.

If the tables had been turned—if I'd been venting to him for fifteen minutes while he stared at me as if he were paying attention to my every word and then told me my hair looked better straight than curly—I would have killed him. But because I did it to him, it caught him off guard. I had always sympathized with his meltdowns before, and he didn't expect the rug pull. Irwin still tells this story and still laughs about it.

————————

For me, men have always been higher-maintenance than women. I know that men believe just the opposite, but they are wrong. Men are work. For instance, it takes more time to make an impression with men than with women. It would be a lot faster if I didn't worry about bruising their masculine pride, but I always worry about that. And I encourage other women to worry about it as well. There is nothing more dangerous than a wounded bull, especially if you are the one who has made him bleed.

The obvious lesson here is that men are hard to direct. This is not news. It's in their DNA. They don't like to be corrected, because it's hard for them to admit that they are wrong. It's also why they don't like to take advice. They don't need your stinking advice. Whether it's your job to manage them as their boss or their equal, you have to find ways to give them direction and advice in a manner that will be accepted. In the final analysis, seduction and manipulation can work, but it's not enough. We also need patience and understanding for when they behave badly, and we need to show respect for them when they behave admirably.

Men have a lot of commendable traits that are worth understanding and even emulating. For example, men have grit. Grit is good. I saw this at all the companies where I worked, not just the boys clubs. The men would make sweeping decisions and, sometimes, *huge* mistakes, but they would manage to recover from them, and even when they couldn't recover, they would still survive and even flourish. Why? Because men admire risk-takers, and they forgive one another when a risk doesn't pan out. The bigger the risk, the more macho a man is . . . to another man.

At first I thought it was strange that men who failed so publicly could turn around and get even better jobs. Then I realized that these men are celebrated for their big thinking, even if it sometimes fails big. High-risk, high-reward people are the ones who build companies and make a difference in the world. Playing it safe never won a war. I know many women who have this kind of grit, too. Some of them are even confident enough to allow their grit to be seen. They're the ones who thrive in boys clubs. Be one of them.

7

Clout Is Great. Get It. Use It.

Clout is a powerful weapon in our arsenal. If only we were better at wielding it! In the dictionary it's defined as "influence or power," but it's really both. Clout is a richly deserved by-product of talent, good judgment, and hard work. It's also the most misunderstood and misused weapon. Women in business don't readily understand the power of clout. We are not shrewd, and for the life of me, I can't figure out why. Are we too fair-minded? Does our rigid sense of fair play get in our way when we play in boys clubs? We are smart, talented, driven, and exceptional in many ways, but if we want to keep climbing that corporate ladder, we need clout and we need to know how to bop people over the head with it from time to time, just so they know that we're around.

In March 2007, three of the most senior McCann women were stranded in São Paulo, Brazil, during an air traffic controllers' strike. They were Carol Smith, worldwide account director for Johnson & Johnson; Devika Bulchandani, New York's director of strategic planning; and me, chairman of New York. We had gone to the airport for a Friday night red-eye back to JFK only to be told thirty minutes before boarding that all flights had been canceled. All of the air traffic controllers were on strike. The airline assured the hundreds of people who were now stuck in the airport that we would be able to retrieve our luggage and that they would help us all find hotel rooms.

The first thing to remember when you are stranded anywhere is never leave your fate to the officials. While I was sleeping in the cab on the way to the airport and Carol was on her phone, Devika was looking out the window and had noticed a Marriott Hotel in Guarulhos. When our flight was canceled, she immediately called her husband, Ash, in Manhattan and asked him to call the Marriott directly and get us three rooms before hundreds of stranded people got the same idea. We collected our luggage and checked into the Marriott one hour after our flight was canceled. We also confirmed our seats for the same flight home the next night. Then we drank some wine, toasted our resourcefulness and grace under pressure, and got a great night's sleep.

The next day we started hearing rumors that the air traffic controllers' strike would extend through Saturday night and maybe even beyond that. We collectively agreed that now was the correct time to panic. Devika had a new business pitch scheduled for Monday and needed to be in the office on Sunday. And Carol and I didn't relish staying at the Guarulhos Marriott—as nice as it was—indefinitely.

"Let's send Michael Roth an e-mail," I suggested. Michael Roth is the CEO of IPG, the giant holding company that owns McCann and hundreds of other communication companies around the world. He is probably one of the five most powerful men in the advertising and communications business. Not too many people send Michael Roth personal e-mail, and especially not on a weekend: certainly not with any hope that he will respond.

"He won't get your e-mail until Monday, when his assistant

prints it out for him and puts it on his desk," both Devika and Carol assured me.

But I disagreed. I knew Michael. He had a BlackBerry-like unit.

If he saw a message from me on a Saturday morning, it would intrigue him enough to read it. Besides, I didn't e-mail him that often—only when there was something really pressing on my mind, like being stranded in Brazil during an air traffic controllers' strike. I also knew that he was sensitive to diversity issues in our business. Since women in important positions were as critical a minority as people of color, I was sure we would get his attention.

So I sent him this e-mail and copied the CEO of McCann (John Dooner), the COO (Eric Keshin), and the president of New York (Brett Gosper).

From: DiSesa, Nina
To: Roth, Michael
Cc: Dooner, John; Keshin, Eric; Gosper, Brett
Sent: Sat Mar 31 10:34:36 2007
Subject: Stranded in Brazil

Dear Michael,

I am stuck in Brazil with Devika Bulchandani and Carol Smith due to an air traffic controllers' strike. Devika has a new business pitch on Monday, and Carol and I need manicures desperately. Is there any way IPG can rescue three important damsels in distress? Certainly, there must be something you can do to help us. We are in an airport Marriott in Guarulhos for crying out loud, and lucky even to have rooms. Tragically, we are not drunk, but we *are* desperate. You don't have that many women that you can afford to lose us. Last time this happened, people were stranded here for TWELVE DAYS. Write soon.

Love,
Nina

Guess who answered my e-mail inside of five minutes? Michael Roth. Within an hour, the most senior executives at IPG were on the case. By Saturday afternoon, they decided that if the strike continued through that night, a private jet would pick us up and take us home—even though they didn't quite know how a private jet could take off if the airport was closed. I assured them that we had seen small, private jets taking off in the morning, but that didn't matter. Rational thought had no place here; this was an emotional situation. It didn't matter to us whether or not they actually *could* rescue us. The important thing was that they *wanted* to rescue us and had acted quickly. We were happy.

On Saturday night the airport opened, and we left Brazil for New York on our previously scheduled flight. Carol, Devika, and I felt mollified because IPG had been willing to come to our rescue, and the men at IPG felt good because they had been ready to rescue us. It worked out well all-around.

But you don't have to be the chairman of a company to have influence. Anyone can get clout if they know where to find it. Consider young Harold.

Harold: Boy Genius

Young Harold was a personal assistant (a.k.a. a secretary) to a very famous commercial film director at a prestigious production company. He never studied psychology to my knowledge, but he was a genius at judging human nature. In a creative environment like film production, his position was traditionally at the bottom of the food chain, but no one thought to mention that to Harold. He was an affable guy, bright-eyed and eager, and everyone liked him upon first contact. But that wasn't enough for him.

Harold wanted power, and he knew how to get it. He did it two ways.

First, he made it his business to understand the film production business just enough to anticipate the needs of the director he assisted. Second, he had brilliant insight and realized that there were many tedious but important jobs that no one wanted to do. So he did them. Harold was shrewd.

Every time something had to be done, Harold was there, either in the process of doing it or assuring everyone that it was already taken care of. This included normal tasks like scheduling meetings with people who didn't want to meet and taking care of everyone's dry-cleaning needs (not just his boss's). It also included genius-caliber tasks like fixing the copy machines when the paper jammed and solving the mystifying computer problems that popped up regularly. Everyone in the company took it for granted that if Harold was in the building, they didn't have to worry about anything.

After Harold had been there for a year or two, no one knew how to do anything. All of the other directors in the company and all of their producers were totally dependent on Harold for the simple things that made their lives worth living. He knew how to get the best coffee and scones with clotted cream delivered within five minutes *and* how to operate the complicated, state-of-the-art video equipment in the conference room. (At McCann, the people who run our video equipment are gods.) Harold knew the best hotels in New York and the head concierge at each of them—and he could get rooms for people when the hotels were booked. He could also get reservations at the best restaurants in New York, L.A., London, and Mumbai, because he knew all the maître d's and maintained e-mail relationships with them. Harold could get a table at Nobu, for crying out loud. The kid was powerful.

Anytime anything had to be done, people would respond with:
"Get Harold!"
"Where's Harold?"
"Harold knows."
And everyone's unanimously favorite response:
"Harold already did it."
One day the president of the company slammed his hand on a

table in a staff meeting and showed how out-of-touch he was with his own company by asking:

"Who the hell is Harold?"

Harold had an office with a window, and he never had to ask for a raise. When the holidays came, he got the most presents, from coworkers, outside vendors, and various clients whom Harold had "taken care of" from time to time. When Harold's boss left that company, he took Harold with him. It was a battle, because while no one mourned the loss of the director, everyone was scared to death of life without Harold. He had become indispensable to the company even though he never even graduated from high school.

Now that's clout.

So how do you get it? Believe me, there are plenty of clout-building opportunities that nobody takes advantage of. Keep your eyes and options open.

My first taste of clout came from food and working on assignments that no one else wanted (Harold's strategy). This is not a bad plan, and it works nicely with the silk purse/sow's ear approach: Make a silk purse from silk and you're a bag-maker. Make one out of a sow's ear and you could have a career in advertising.

If you see an opportunity to shine, grab it—especially if there's no one else around reaching for it. I got my start with three Ps: Pasta, Peas, and Pops.

Pasta: When I arrived at Young & Rubicam, my first job at a big New York ad agency, my first assignment was for Chef Boyardee Canned Spaghetti. It seemed that every creative person who came to Y&R at the entry level was assigned to Chef Boyardee. It was either a rite of passage or a baptism by fire, depending on your success. Over the years, the Chef became more relevant with the introduction of new products, but when I was working on the brand, it was a tough sell. It was difficult for an Italian American like me to be sincere about the "goodness" in canned spaghetti. I never knew spaghetti even came in a can. At least, it never did in my house. What made this an even tougher assignment was that a test score was the measure of success. I had never heard of the notion of testing creative work before it ran. That's a big-agency phenomenon, because big agencies have big clients who expect big results.

The reason we test commercials for products that are mass-marketed is the media cost. A big consumer brand like Chef Boyardee could have an annual media budget anywhere from $20 million to $100 million or more, and most of it is still spent on TV and print. Add the cost of producing those TV commercials, and you have a sizable financial commitment. Clients naturally want to make sure that a commercial will be effective before they spend their money. So they test. The agency creates a commercial in a "rough" form with animated drawings and a soundtrack that come as close as possible to what the finished spot will look and sound like. Then we show it to a cross section of people to find out if the spot was noticed, remembered, and liked, and if it made the product desirable enough to purchase.

Clients with mass-marketed products rely heavily on this kind of testing, but creative people hate it. Testing can be the biggest barrier to producing truly unique ideas, because they might have to be viewed more than once to resonate. And that is all we care about as writers and art directors: producing commercials for our reel so we can win awards or get the next big job and eventually become a creative director. This does not change until we actually *become* a creative director and shoulder the responsibility of our clients' business results. And honestly, for some creative directors, it doesn't change even then.

Chef Boyardee had been a challenge for Y&R for a while, even before I arrived. I think the common belief at Y&R was that if they put enough bodies on a difficult assignment, someday someone would crack the code. None of us minded, because if *we* were the ones to crack it, *we'd be heroes,* and heroes have clout.

After several weeks of fumbling around on this assignment, I finally wrote a commercial the clients bought, and it went in for testing. When the results came back, the associate creative director on the business came into my office with astonishing news.

"Congratulations," he said with a big smile. "Your Chef Boyardee spot just came back with the highest recall score of any TV spot they've ever tested on the business."

"No shit!"

"Yeah," he said, laughing. "More than ninety-six percent of the people who saw it remembered it."

"Ninety-six percent? NINETY-SIX PERCENT?"

"Yeah."

"OHMYGOD. When do we go into production?" I asked, fantasizing about my first trip to Los Angeles. L-*frigging*-A. La-la land— the coveted, glamorous production location for everyone back in the eighties. (This was before I realized I didn't look good in L.A.) Y&R practically *owned* the famed Beverly Hills Hotel. In my first few weeks at the agency, I had heard stories about how creative people and producers would hang out at the hotel's restaurant, The Polo Lounge, and rub elbows with Hollywood's elite. How they would spend their downtime lounging at the hotel's famous pool, where a big Swede named Sven doted on you with fresh drinks and clean towels.

Everything sort of went out of focus and I started to hyperventilate—until the creative director snapped me back to reality.

"Don't pack," he said. Now he was choking in anticipation of his revelation.

In addition to the highest recall of 96.4 percent, my commercial also had the highest aggravation score.

"Aggravation?" I didn't get it.

"The reason it had such high recall," the creative director explained, "is that everyone who saw the spot hated and despised it."

"Everyone?"

"Well, ninety-four percent of the ninety-six percent who remembered it. But congratulations. Nobody has ever gotten such high 'dislike' numbers either. You broke two records."

"Does that mean we won't be producing it?" What was so great about being liked? I *hated* most of the commercials I saw on TV.

The creative director left my office laughing hysterically.

The only silver lining to this story is that my brain has taken pity on me, and now I can't even remember what that spot was about. I know there was a lot of repetition in it. That was what made the commercial so memorable. And so damned annoying, too.

For a week or two I became notorious throughout the creative department for that rare and humiliating testing achievement. It was not the fame I'd been hoping for, and yet for one brief, shining moment, it appeared that I had made it, that in just five weeks I had done something that no one else at Y&R had been able to do in *two years.*

What a coup it would have been.

What respect I could have won, what admiration.

What *clout!*

If only that damned spot had been good.

Peas: I labored for a few more months on canned spaghetti, and then one day someone came into my life and saved my sanity. Michael Hampton, another associate creative director in my group, had heard about my brush with success with Chef Boyardee. (Even a spectacular failure can be good for something, as being infamous is almost as good as being famous.) It turns out he was in desperate need of help with Birds Eye Frozen Garden Peas. All of the radio spots for the product had just been killed, and he needed a new campaign in two days. He probably figured that, given the unfortunate outcome of the Chef Boyardee incident, I had plenty of time on my hands. He wanted to know if I had any experience with writing radio commercials. I told him I had written a few (like a few hundred or so), and that I'd give peas a shot.

All my training at Howard Marks kicked in, and I wrote an amusing campaign about people called "The Fresh Averse." They recoiled at anything fresh, and they especially hated fresh *peas*. ("So much work," they would whine about the shelling process. "And for what? A piddling little *pea*?") The Fresh Averse only wanted frozen vegetables. In one spot, people broke out in a fist-fight over Birds Eye Frozen Peas because they tasted *too* fresh. "Are you pulling a fast one?" they asked, and then all hell broke loose. For a good fifteen seconds there was no dialogue—just fighting sound effects and grunts. It was silly but funny, and the clients liked it. And since all the humor was focused on the product, the campaign tested really well, and after that the clients *loved* it.

This was my first lesson in winning at the testing game. It turned out to be easy. Just make sure the surprise and humor is focused on the product, because when people remember the jokes, they'll remember the product. This seems obvious, but there are still creative people who don't get the logic, even when I tell them the secret. They fail in testing, and then they complain that testing kills good work. It rarely killed my good work, and throughout my career I became skilled at getting high test scores for the clients who would allow me to use humor.

After the success of the Birds Eye radio spots, it was all over the agency that some new writer from "the South" (they remembered Richmond and forgot I came from Brooklyn) had written and *sold* a funny radio campaign for *frozen peas,* and suddenly I was no longer lost in the sea of twelve hundred Y&R employees. I became in hot demand throughout the creative department, and creative directors asked me to work on the most boring assignments in the hopes that

I could make them interesting. The last straw came when one of them asked if I could write an outdoor billboard for an insurance company. He wanted something riveting, competitive, insightful, hard-hitting yet warm, human, and aimed at women.

"Oh, and remember this, kiddo." (I was hot, but he couldn't remember my name.) "It's *outdoors*. Cars are whizzing by at fifty-five miles per hour. No more than seven words. If you can do it in five—stupendous."

I begged Michael Hampton to *"get me outta this,"* and luckily, he was in need of my services again.

Pops: Michael had just sold a TV commercial that was a big musical extravaganza to introduce a new product for General Foods called Jell-O Gelatin Pops. I didn't know much about TV commercials at the time, but even to my untrained eye this one looked like a disaster. It featured unconnected scenes (those dratted vignettes) of various people eating Jell-O Gelatin Pops on the beach and singing—in *rhyme*—all of the copy points that made this product desirable: refreshing, cool, fruity. AUUUGGGHHH! It was awful.

Much to Michael's dismay, this commercial had tested the best out of all of the ideas he had presented (no one could figure out why), and he was stuck with producing it. He asked me to cover the shoot with him, because the guy who'd written the damned spot had had enough good sense to resign. This was my first trip to L.A.—The Big Time—and I was the surrogate copywriter for a commercial I would have never created in a million years. Even back then, I didn't do jingles and I hated vignettes.

What made matters even worse, if that was possible, was that we had to film this in December, and even though it was L.A., it was freezing on the beach. The girls in bathing suits had goose bumps all over their bodies, so during the close-ups we had to have heaters everywhere, and because there were so many of them everyone kept tripping on them, and they kept breaking down.

But here is the absolute worst part of this story: For some reason, the damned *finished* commercial didn't test as well as the animated test spot did, which proves that if an idea isn't good to begin with, one-dimensional people will be more interesting than real human beings. The client was both appalled and confused, and they joined Michael and me in our hatred of the spot. Now we were out of time. The product was scheduled for distribution in March, and we had no advertising to introduce it. Something had to be on the air by March 1—and it was the end of January.

Michael was under the gun to come up with a big idea, and fast. He thought he had one, but he needed a good writer to help him pull it off. That writer turned out to be me. The idea was to recreate *The Little Rascals* and to use our versions of Alfalfa,* Buckwheat, Darla, Spanky, Froggy, and Pete the dog to sell the new pops. The idea could go either way. If the spots were written and cast well and directed flawlessly, they could become a famous campaign. Any slipups and we would have another embarrassment on our hands. What gave me courage was that I knew I could write cute copy for kids, and I had total confidence in Michael's production skills and taste as an art director.

"The Little Rascals" was my first big foray into the power of "cute." We had five six-year-olds and a dog. And we were talking to moms. Come on, it's almost cheating. What mother could resist a gang of adorable kids discovering Jell-O Gelatin Pops and then inventing mischievous ways to sell them? They were always getting into trouble with another ongoing character, the Grocery Man, who wanted to sell the pops in his store. Naturally, he took exception to the Rascals' business plan of selling Jell-O Gelatin Pops on the street. It didn't matter that the kids ate more pops

---

* For this part we hired a young Seth Green, who has since grown up to be a talented, successful, and rather handsome young man. When we cast him, he was peculiar-looking enough to make a great Alfalfa.

than they sold; they still annoyed the Grocery Man. He was always chasing them, and they would always find ingenious ways to subvert him and set up their pop stands when he wasn't looking.

The campaign was very effective, and it ran for several years. It won creative awards and a very prestigious marketing award called a Gold Effie. Since Michael was the associate creative director, he got most of the credit for the success—which he deserved—but I got some clout from the job, too. It wasn't a lot, but it was enough at the time. It got me my next big opportunity at Y&R.

Right after our success with "The Little Rascals," the agency reorganized and I was moved to another group. This was when I would first work for John Nieman, a man who would become one of my very best friends personally and professionally. John was the fair-haired boy of the Y&R creative department, and it was a real coup to be chosen to work in his group. (I believe I can thank peas and pops for this break.) It was John who paired me with Frank "The Madman" Costantini, a rising star in the creative department and my nemesis until we learned to love each other.

After our Cheetos triumph, Frank and I became one of the hot creative teams at Y&R, and we were developing a reputation for being funny and fast. In addition to our regular assignments, we were constantly being loaned out to "save the day" for other businesses. People would give us an assignment on a Friday and look for work on Monday. They would play to our egos by using one of my own S&M techniques, saying things like, "If you can't crack this problem in two days, no one can."

Any normal person could see this for what it was: heavy-handed manipulation. As an accomplished manipulator myself, I knew what they were up to. But it's hard enough to solve a problem creatively in two days when you know the business and the client. When you're brought in as gunslingers, it's nearly impossible to hit the ground with guns blazing and hope to hit the target. Frank, however, was a sucker for this kind of ego stroking. He

would say, "If we can crack this over the weekend, *we'll be heroes*!"
And hero status paid off in clout.

Even I couldn't resist this kind of exploitation, and Frank and I
always took the bait. Sometimes we would hit a home run and
sometimes we would fail, but no one seemed to remember our
strikeouts. As long as our ideas were intelligent, it didn't seem to
matter whether they sold or not. Y&R was like that back then.

During our brief partnership, Frank and I became a go-to team
of the highest order. We sold and produced an average of fifteen
television commercials per year. This was a big number for a single creative team. It meant we were always shooting. Frank practically lived in L.A., prepping and filming our TV commercials. I
always came for the minimum amount of days. L.A. was too sunny
and pleasant for my taste, and too laid-back. And everyone drove
expensive red convertibles. So *not* New York.

During those highly productive years, the agency promoted me
from copywriter to senior copywriter, and then to creative super-
visor. But my ultimate goal was to be the first female group creative director at Y&R, and to get there I had to make money for the
company. The only way to do that was to run a business on my
own as an associate creative director. So I made the decision to do
something rash. I decided to speak up.

I told John Nieman that my ambition was to become a group
creative director in three years. Then I gave him a gentle but open-
ended ultimatum: If the agency didn't plan my career, then I
would have to plan it myself. And if that happened, my career path
might not be restricted to Y&R.

I had never done anything like this before, but that meeting was
a watershed moment for me. It was the first time I had ever asked
for anything in a firm, straightforward manner. It was definitely a
meeting between Nieman and my inner guy. I remember how surprised he was to have that conversation with me. Stunned, almost.
But part of my courage came from confidence. Nieman liked me,

and since the work that Frank and I did was often put on the agency show reel, I was hoping he didn't want to lose me.

Shortly after that chat, my opportunity showed up. The Kentucky Fried Chicken business went "on notice." That meant store sales were down, the franchisees were up in arms, and our agency needed to fix the problem quickly. Nieman made me an offer that I couldn't refuse, even though it scared the daylights out of me. He said that if I saved the KFC account, he would make me an associate creative director and I could run the business. He gave me ninety days to fix it.

As an "acting" associate creative director, I put several teams on the KFC assignment and guided the creative process by looking at work, brainstorming ideas, and upgrading the work others did (helping good ideas to become better). This is what a creative director is supposed to do. It was what I had learned from Michael Hampton and other good creative directors. Over a course of six weeks, I presented a total of ten campaigns to the KFC clients. Some of them were actually very good, but the clients didn't buy anything and I was running out of time. I had no choice. I had to work on the assignment myself and compete with the very people who were working *for* me.

This is a last-resort strategy. Good creative directors, like all good leaders, are not supposed to compete with the people who work for them. If it's done on a regular basis, we are roundly criticized, and if we get a reputation for only selling our own work or for taking credit for other people's ideas, pretty soon the stars in the agency will refuse to work for us. If that happens, we can't succeed. But I had been nurturing, supportive, and collaborative long enough. It was the eleventh hour and I had to take over, show some grit, roll the dice. In other words, I had to act like a man.

In order to do this, though, I needed my old partner back. Unfortunately, while I was off being an acting creative director, Frank had paired up with another partner, and he didn't have the time or the incentive to help me crack KFC. No one was going to make *him* an associate creative director. I had to appeal to his feelings for me and his ever-pressing need for hero status. We never outgrow that need, thank God.

I convinced him to help me by assuring him that he was so good, we could probably crack it over the weekend (male pride), and that if we did crack it, he would gain hero status like never before (male ego). I booked a room at a nice hotel and told Frank he could order anything he wanted from room service (he loved room service), but that we couldn't sleep until we had the Big Idea.

At Y&R, the creative directors with enough clout could spend the agency's money at their own discretion. For example, if we worked late, we could order mountains of food from the local deli and put it on the agency's account. And if a business was in trouble, we could stash creative teams in hotel rooms with unlimited room service so they could work 24/7 without interruptions. The "hotel stash" was a true test of power because, as long as we didn't abuse this privilege, we could act first and get approval after the fact. It was one of the benefits of working for a privately owned company that made a lot of money. (Y&R is not privately owned anymore.)

Our hotel weekend paid off. In two days we created the campaign for KFC that would turn their business around. Here was their problem and our solution:

McDonald's had just come out with Chicken McNuggets, and this was KFC's biggest nightmare: going head-to-head with the Golden Arches. Chicken McNuggets were meant to compete squarely with KFC, and for the first time, the company that "did chicken right" was worried. McDonald's was encroaching on KFC's turf. It was not only aggravating for KFC, it was embarrassing, because McDonald's had beaten KFC to the punch and introduced chicken nuggets first. Our strategy was to try to discredit McDonald's as a chicken expert and thereby question the "quality" of its product without actually saying anything bad about it. Note: It is not allowed to openly trash a competitor's product. The networks will not run an ad that is in any way disparaging toward another company. You can gently poke fun at a competitor, but even if it's legal, you run the risk of consumer backlash. They could hate your brand and support could swing over to your competition. When you see an ad that does go head-on against a competitor, you'll notice there is a lot of charm and gentle humor.

Using a new technique called clay animation, or Claymation, we created a character we nicknamed Baby, because conceiving him was quick and fun (and it happened in a hotel room), but bringing him to life (getting the idea approved) was a long and painful process that took almost *nine months.*

Baby had a hamburger body with a chicken's head, legs, and wings. He represented a hamburger who tried to look and act like a chicken but always failed in a cute and disarming way. Baby sounds gross, but he was really adorable, and this little guy sold the hell out of KFC's chicken nuggets. It was groundbreaking then because it was the first time that KFC had gone after McDonald's, even though we never mentioned that company's name or showed its golden arches. But because the highly competitive campaign was done with so much charm, there was no backlash from the consumers. Instead, it made them laugh.

Another unexpected benefit of our campaign was that, instead of cannibalizing KFC's boned chicken business (i.e., converting boned sales to nugget sales—not a great way to make money), the nugget sales were incremental and the campaign improved KFC's entire business. And this was during a period when the entire fast food industry was suffering depressed numbers.

Frank and I were heroes!

The campaign saved the account for Y&R and ran for two years. Frank and I got raises, and I was made an associate creative director. KFC gave me my first taste of rainmaker clout. And it was finger-lickin' good.

Use It or Lose It

Having clout is only half the battle. It must be used and invested wisely and with integrity. If you do this right, more clout will come your way. Every once in a while, test the waters by asking for something you want but don't necessarily deserve. Men are good at this. They ask for things they don't deserve all the time, and they get them. Things like more important jobs, bigger raises, larger offices, loftier titles. Men like living large.

I know one man who is a master at acquiring perks and promotions he doesn't deserve (even he is surprised when his employers meet his most outrageous requests). He gets away with it because he makes money for the firm, plus he is charming and a good talker. His company even pays for his expensive and prestigious country-club membership, where he plays golf with one client *once a year*. The rest of the time it's for his personal use. And he's the only one in this company who has this perk other than the CEO and CFO.

But clout is not just valuable for getting promotions and perks. It can also protect you from all sorts of professional unpleasantness. For instance, when I was a group creative director at McCann we had a cigarette account in the system, and I didn't want to work on cigarettes. I had enough clout with the agency to beg off that business and not be penalized for it.

Clout can protect you from hidden dangers as well. Women have a tough time in male-dominated cultures, and young, attractive women have even more problems. Men hit on them. A woman named Frances worked for fourteen years in the classic boys club of network news. At her office, the resident Don Juan had made a play for every attractive woman in sight—for fourteen years. He hit on everyone except her. The day she left, she walked into his office to say good-bye. He was, as always, gracious and respectful to her. After wishing him well, she started to leave but then walked back to his desk.

"I'm not asking for a date or anything," Frances said to him. "I just want to know, for my own curiosity, why you never hit on *me*." And he said with a grin, "Are you kidding? I was terrified of you."

Why was he afraid to approach her? She was certainly attractive. Hell, I would have hit on her if I were a guy. But something stopped this man from messing around with her. He just wouldn't risk it. She still says she doesn't know why, but I'll make a wild guess and say that she was too important to the company to risk losing her.

And that brings me to my last two observations about clout.

If you use clout with honor, it can make you a better person and a stronger leader. Used incorrectly, it can make you an obnoxious, self-serving, loathsome asshole. You need to make this choice carefully. Once you become known as an obnoxious, self-serving, loathsome asshole, that will stay with you for life.

And lastly, be careful that someone doesn't turn the tables on you and club you with their own clout. Beware of the Clout Louts.

The Dark Side of Clout

Clout Louts have despicable behavior. They use their influence and power to blackmail their company and get perks they don't deserve. If they have a special relationship with an important client, for instance, they can make demands on their employer for undeserved raises and promotions and get away with it. There is a lot of resentment toward the people who do this, but Clout Louts are so narcissistic, they don't even notice or care.

The most despicable Clout Louts are the predators. These are often men with so much power, they are virtually untouchable, meaning they can do almost anything they please without re-proach. One of the worst things they can do is hit on young, de-fenseless women in the company, especially the ones who work directly *for* them. Interestingly, they never hit on the women they *need*, only on the ones they can easily replace. These are usually the youngest women, who have not yet made their mark in the company. They are the most vulnerable and the easiest to take ad-vantage of. Men who prey on defenseless women are cowards.

When I first started working in advertising, it was not uncom-mon for men in important positions to sexually harass these younger, vulnerable women. I'm not talking about real affairs of the heart; I mean giving *unwanted* attention. Now, this problem has gotten so expensive (more than twelve thousand sexual ha-rassment lawsuits were filed in 2006*) that most companies have enforced compliance. Employees have to attend seminars clearly stating the policies of decorum and what constitutes sexual harass-ment. McCann Erickson takes this issue *very* seriously. In addition, more and more companies are requiring colleagues who are hav-ing a consensual relationship to sign a "love contract" to protect the company from a future sexual harassment lawsuit.

The result of all these precautions is that sexual harassment today has gone underground. It's not as blatant, but it still exists. Christmas parties can be the worst, and even classy shops have horror stories of men (usually creative directors, I'm sorry to say) doing lewd things in public in front of and often with young women. I heard one story of a very senior and well-respected cre-ative director who got drunk at one Christmas party and kept hit-ting on women with his dick hanging out of his pants. It wasn't even in a box! Unfortunately, the women who fall victim to such bad behavior don't have clout in the agency.

Let's talk about affairs of the heart for a moment. In general, it

* As reported on NBC's *Today Show* on July 5, 2007.

is never a good idea to fall under the spell of the office Lothario, whether he is your boss or not, even if you think you are sophisticated enough to handle it. With office romances, the woman is usually the one to leave when the affair ends, because the man invariably carries more clout.

Here's an uncanny truism about office romances: When you are in love, you will never run into each other. Once you break up, your ex-lover will be in every single elevator you walk into. It's some kind of twisted Murphy's Law.

I have seen women who were old enough to know better derailed by "interacting" with their boss or other male colleagues in high positions. Protect yourself by not getting involved with men who can hurt you, or by earning enough clout so that these men hold you in high esteem. A man will not jeopardize his position if he is afraid of the repercussions. This is another reason for being driven to make money for the company: No one messes around with a rainmaker.

When women find themselves in precarious situations with men in the office, they often come to me in an unofficial capacity. One young woman was upset because her very influential boss made her "uncomfortable." He was always asking her personal questions about whom she was dating and where she was going. He would compliment her on her clothes every day, telling her why he liked an outfit and how well she wore it. I wasn't sure if this man was making a play for her or not. He probably was, but there was always the slight chance that he genuinely liked her, and this was just his way of demonstrating it. Still, he outranked her *and* he had a reputation for interoffice affairs, so she didn't trust his intentions.

I wanted to give him the benefit of the doubt, but even more, she needed to get enough control over her predicament so that she wouldn't become a chronic victim. I told her that I could intercede on her behalf, but that it would be better if she handled it on her own. She had to learn how to protect herself so that if this ever happened again, she could nip it in the bud and keep her self-respect. I told her to go into her boss's office, close the door, and stand in front of him. It was important for her not to sit down. If she stood he would have to look *up* to *her.*

Then I told her to tell him, very calmly, that when he asks personal questions about her private life, it makes her *very uncomfortable.* When he comments on her clothes, even though she is sure he means it as a compliment, it makes her *very uncomfortable.* I told her to use this phrase several times, because she would be sending him a signal. An unwelcome comment that makes a subordinate feel "*very uncomfortable*" is one of the legal definitions of sexual harassment. By doing this, she would send him a code that meant she knew she had the agency and the law on her side, and he was treading on dangerous territory. But she needed to do it in a nonthreatening, nonaggressive way. And by not directly accusing him of anything, she would give him a graceful way out.

To this man's credit, he immediately apologized and said he was unaware that he was making her feel uncomfortable. He just liked her and thought he was being supportive. He said he would stop, and he did. Immediately. He didn't get into trouble, and she didn't get fired or feel pressured into resigning. But most of all, she felt empowered, and she learned how to start taking care of her own needs. This young woman put herself in a good position, and soon after this incident she had enough self-confidence to start earning some of her own clout.

But why is it so hard for women to stand up for themselves? Not just with bullies, but even with people who can do us some good? What is it about our nature that makes us so humble? Why can't we learn how to accept praise and promote ourselves? Men do it all the time. Watch them. Learn from them.

8

The Seven Deadly Sins in Boys Clubs

If you're working with alpha men in any kind of culture, steer clear of the pitfalls that will obviously label you as someone they will want to shun. The Seven Deadly Sins to avoid are:

Humility

Timidity

Cowardice

Submissiveness

Blind Obedience

Visible Fear

Hypersensitivity

There are more sins, but I'm doing a "seven" thing here. Most of these sins can be avoided if we just muster up enough confidence to *stand up and be counted, damn it!*

For some reason, it's challenging for us to be our own champions. It's not difficult for men, but it's almost impossible for even the most accomplished women. We need to stand up in a lot of ways: to get attention, to receive and *accept* praise, to deflate bullies, and sometimes just to be heard. No matter how smart we are or how driven, if we are quiet achievers, we will never get ahead in the company of men.

I always wonder why women don't brag. Do you even *know* a successful man in business who doesn't brag about himself or take credit for his achievements? Even the unsuccessful ones do it. Are most women just too shy to take credit for the things we do, or is there something genetically wrong with us? And, as if a brag-challenged brain isn't bad enough, when someone heaps praise on us, what do we do? We immediately refuse any responsibility for our success. *We deflect glory.*

One of my nicest clients pulled off a huge coup on an assignment that had produced nothing but public failure in the past. Her boss called her in to his office to give her a bonus (which she accepted, thank God. I would have had to kill her if she deflected the *money*), but she couldn't accept the praise.

I hear about women doing this all of the time. They say:

"I had a great team on my side."

No kidding. Who doesn't have a great team?

"I couldn't have done it alone."

No *kidding.* No one does anything alone in business.

"My team deserves all the credit."

Ouch, ouch, OUCH!

What does a man say when someone tells him he did a great job?

A man says, *"Thank you."*

Stand in front of a mirror and practice saying these words over and over again until it becomes second nature:

"Thank you."

"Thank you, I'm very happy to have contributed."

"Thank you. Thank you very much."

"It was a lot of work, but I'm glad it paid off."

Forget altruism. You have to be *seen* and your efforts have to be *recognized* so that you can get the credit you deserve. You want that spotlight aimed squarely at you. After all, it's a double-edged sword. If you're in a management position, you will be as visible when you fail as when you knock it out of the park. People won't pull their punches if you *don't* succeed. Those blows will land squarely on you, and you will bruise. Why not take the strokes as well as the blows?

There are a lot of ways to get credit for what you have accomplished, but it will never happen if no one hears you. This was the case with my friend Allison, the CEO of a small but important company. Allison is a very accomplished woman who has several strikes against her: she is beautiful, she has a great body, and she looks easily ten years younger than her real age of forty-two. She is highly respected in her company and the people who know her admire her, yet strangers found it easy to dismiss her. I didn't realize this until we started taking meetings together.

We were serving on the board of a highly respected nonprofit organization, and we were the only women among about eighteen high-powered men. The men dominated these meetings, and if you had something to say, it was very hard to get their attention. It was less hard for me, because I had my training with boys clubs and knew how to get men to listen (I yell at them, literally), but Allison was in the dark.

As the head of a company, she wasn't accustomed to being ignored, and she didn't know how to command a room filled with people who didn't work for her. Every time she'd start to say something, one of the men would start talking over her and everyone would look at him instead of her. She did this several times until we all left the meeting during a break. Since Allison and I were alone in the ladies' room, she was finally able to say her piece.

"They are so fucking RUDE!" my quiet friend yelled to me from inside the stall she was using. "I fucking can't *believe* it. What a bunch of *assholes.* I CAN'T GET A WORD IN EDGEWISE WITH THOSE . . . *JERKS.*"

Holy shit, where did all this spunk come from? Allison was on *fire.*

I told her that if she spoke up that loudly in the meeting, half her problems would be solved. I said that I didn't think the men were consciously being rude to her, they just didn't see or *hear* her. Even I hadn't been able to hear her, and I had strained to listen.

"You have to take command of the room," I told her. "Stand up, speak clearly, project your voice, and always begin by saying something charming or disarming before you speak your mind. Just try to get them to laugh, and they'll pay attention to you." I gave her a line to use, and when we went back to the meeting, she tried it the next time she had something to say.

"Gentlemen," Allison said, interrupting a spirited conversation by standing up. "Your discussion is so riveting, I forgot what I wanted to say." Beat pause. The men looked at her in surprise, but even more important, they were *speechless.* "Oh, wait a second," she said, grinning. "I just remembered. It's this . . ." And she made her points and sat down.

When Allison had stood up, sure enough, the men stopped talking and looked at her. They laughed at her joke, and when she started to speak her mind, they all listened to her. They *enjoyed* listening to her. (She's not only beautiful, but she's smart—did I say that already?) They smiled at her while she was talking, and some of them actually agreed with her.

This is the way it goes with men sometimes: They laugh, they listen, and then they are on your side. You have charmed them. It's a good combination, and it almost always works.

A quick laugh has a lot of benefits. First, your "joke" doesn't really need to be all that funny, just a little out of character for the person delivering it. Everyone knew that Allison hadn't forgotten what she wanted to say, but she was normally so serious that her playful remark stopped the men cold. It also didn't hurt her to speak loudly. That's how men talk to one another. If you want to play with them, you have to speak up. You're not going to get any credit for anything if they can't even hear you. So *roar.*

Unfortunately, just being able to speak above the din isn't enough when you're trying to get the attention of the men you work with. Young women especially tend to get very frustrated when no one notices that they are doing a good job and they are too low on the totem pole to do anything about it. What does one do when this happens, I am often asked? Get a third party involved.

One of the interesting idiosyncrasies of human nature is that we tend to respect the opinions of people who don't give a rat's ass about an outcome. We always listen to an objective third party because he or she has no hidden agenda. So find a buddy who is objective and let this person toot your horn for you. The buddy system works two ways. First, you can find someone at the office on the same level as you and come to a "reciprocal praise agreement." Your buddy will let people know about your successes in subtle, believable ways, and you will do the same for her (or him). You don't want to choose someone who is less respected than you are—that praise won't be meaningful to your boss. You also don't want someone who is too far ahead of you, because your praise for her (or him) may not be as meaningful.

The second way to do this is to have a champion in a higher position; someone who has nothing to gain from promoting your cause and doesn't expect anything in return. Just be careful that your champion is not so high on the food chain that you become a "special-interest candidate," someone who is perceived to be undeserving of special attention. It could backfire, and you could garner resentment.

Either way, acknowledgment of your work from an objective third party has to be handled delicately. You can't just charge ahead like a bull in a china shop. Find the right stimulus to get the response you are looking for.

Before I became anyone's boss, I worked with a brilliant young woman named Sarah who was being overlooked by her superiors. We would be in a meeting and a problem would come up that Sarah had already detected and even found a possible solution for, but no one would listen. What could I do on Sarah's behalf?

"Well," I said to the group the next time this happened. "Sarah and I were eating lunch the other day, and she had a great suggestion for this very thing. It's so brilliant, I'd be taking credit for it myself if she wasn't sitting right here." Then I looked at her and said, "Do you want to go to the bathroom so I can hog the spotlight, or do you want to tell them yourself?"

Naturally, everyone was eager to hear Sarah's idea. But there was something else that was accomplished subliminally. It didn't hurt either of us to drop the hint that we talk about business while we're eating lunch.

There are other ways to bolster someone's standing, like with this offhanded remark:

"You know, that strategy Lisa wrote was so good, the creative people showed her their work before they showed it to Mike [the creative director]. Don't tell him, though, because he'll be pissed that a strategic planner has that much clout with creative people."

Just saying she came up with a good strategy would be meaningless and subjective, but saying the creative people—those rigid, arrogant purists—respected a planner enough to voluntarily show her their creative work was an *achievement*. Lisa had won their admiration because she was smart and gave them a strategy with brilliant consumer insights. She made the creative people look good *and* didn't take direct credit for her contributions. A double whammy. The fact that the creative people showed her their work before they showed it to the creative director was a huge compliment, and an objective third party giving her some credit completed the circle.

Perception vs. Reality

One of the only advantages of getting older (other than the fact that you haven't died yet) is that you appear to have all the answers. Still, it took a long time for me to fully appreciate the psychology of business. Until I saw the light, I always believed that if I simply put my nose to the grindstone and worked hard, my efforts would be appreciated and I would be noticed. I believed that I didn't have to toot my own horn. I was not shrewd. Even worse, I was a sucker.

But somewhere along the way, I had an epiphany: Perception doesn't just trump reality, in most cases, perception *is* reality.

My friend B. J. Kaplan and I were both writers at Young & Rubicam at the beginning of our careers. We had both come from small, out-of-town agencies, and Y&R was our first big New York agency job. B.J. had already been there for almost two years when I arrived, and she had earned a very solid creative reputation. By the time I got there, she was known for her quirky personality, her quick sense of humor, and her ability to create good work that clients loved. Everyone liked her, she was prolific, and she was always in demand. She was the darling of the creative group where she was assigned.

I was assigned to the same group and decided immediately that I liked her. But it was impossible to get her attention. She wouldn't have lunch with me ("No time for lunch," she said. "Too busy."), and I could barely get her to talk to me. It couldn't have been that she didn't like me because she didn't even know me. I was convinced that B.J.'s "friend ship" must have been filled to capacity, and that if she added me, the whole thing would sink.

"You're like Audrey Hepburn," I told her one day, when she was once again too busy to have lunch with me.

That got her attention. She thought I meant she was thin.

"You know, like in that opening scene in *Charade*,* when she meets Cary Grant for the first time."

GRANT: Do we know each other?
HEPBURN: Why? You think we're going to?
GRANT: I don't know. How would I know?
HEPBURN: Because I already know an awful lot of people, and until one of them dies, I couldn't possibly meet anyone else.
GRANT: Hmm. Well, if anyone goes on the critical list, let me know.
HEPBURN: Quitter.

I always loved that film. So did B.J. But even at that, it took an entire summer to win her over. We would sun on the roof of the apartment building where we both lived and talk about advertising, the pros and cons of tanning machines, and how infuriating unrequited love was. Eventually, we started girl-dating. This is what single women do when we are between men.

B.J. and I would spend every Saturday together. First we'd get a manicure and then we'd have lunch at some trendy restaurant. Sometimes we'd go to a movie. We saw *Moonstruck* three times in one week during a Christmas holiday, even though B.J. hates romantic comedies. Often we would buy things we didn't need, or get a makeup makeover at Saks Fifth Avenue. We were not good drinkers, and even one glass of an amusing white wine could impair our judgment. Once, right after we got our annual bonus checks, we celebrated with *two* glasses of wine and bought our first fur coats right off the rack at Bloomingdale's. We wore them out of the store. It was the best feeling.

* Written by Peter Stone and Marc Behm.

Soon I made it my responsibility to help B.J. broaden her horizons. I thought she was too self-involved and needed something in her life that would be just as important to her as she was. I started small. First, I enriched her life with a ficus plant. When she didn't kill it, I gave her a parakeet for her birthday. Then one Saturday we saw *The Witches of Eastwick* and we loved that scene where Cher, Susan Sarandon, and Michelle Pfeiffer get drunk off Martinis. We also loved the *glasses,* so after the film we went to Barneys and bought some. Then we stopped at a bar and had two huge Martinis on empty stomachs.

The next thing we remembered was being in a pet store on Lexington Avenue. An hour later, I stuffed B.J. into a cab loaded down with a scratching post, a litter pan, bags of litter, cans of cat food, and a tiny Siamese kitten. She woke up on Sunday morning with a furry little ball mewing in her ear, and it was the first time she remembered what we had done. She named the bit of fluff Oliver, and he became the love of her life.

But in spite of our solid friendship, my presence at Y&R started to make B.J. reassess her role at the agency. She was beginning to notice that I seemed to have more clout than she did. In a relatively short time, I had earned a good creative reputation with my "Three Ps" (Pasta, Peas, and Pops), and soon I had gained my great partner, Frank Costantini, which helped me get even more clout.

But B.J. had a list of her own achievements and was working with a great art director, too. In fact, she did a lot *more* work than I did. Why did I appear to have more respect in her mind? What was the difference?

It turned out that the culprit was all perception.

In business, it is common practice to give the busiest people the most critical assignments. They are not busy for nothing, since they are usually the more talented people; and they will get the job done, since they are also more driven. And that's what would happen with B.J. and me and our respective art directors/partners. An account management team would come into our offices (often at eight o'clock at night, when we were already working late for someone else) and make an unreasonable request. First of all, we weren't supposed to take assignments from account managers, only from our group creative directors, so the rules were being broken to begin with. But the account management team would break protocol anyway and come by to sweet-talk us into helping them. B.J. would give them a pained, grimacelike smile and agree to take the assignment, even though it meant working even more nights and weekends.

Conversely, I always reacted differently, especially at eight o'clock in the frigging evening.

"Gee, I'm sorry, but that's out of the question," I would say with great sincerity. "We would gladly help, but Frank and I are so buried right now, we're already busy working every weekend. Right, Frank?"

Frank would be skulking around in my office while this was going on, clearly bored with the conversation and checking his receding hairline in the mirror behind my desk.

"FRANK."

He was terrible at this game, being totally guileless, and when I said things like this, he would just smirk and try not to giggle. He knew I would kill him if he laughed.

"We're so *crazed,* we can't even think straight," I would add. "You don't want *half a brain* working on your assignment, do you?"

Of course they did. They were account managers. For them, half a creative brain was better than nothing, and they wouldn't have bothered coming to us at eight o'clock at night, risking the wrath of our creative director, if they weren't desperate.

After my sweet refusal, they would slink out of my office mumbling something like, "Well, do the best you can. Anything would be appreciated."

Then Frank and I would work all weekend and give them

something great. So would B.J. and her partner. But guess who got the most credit and certainly more gratitude? And guess which team got more clout for "coming through in a pinch"? The squeaky wheels—Frank and me.

I told B.J. she was too accommodating, and that people took her efforts for granted.

"Let people know you had to make sacrifices to accommodate them and they will value you more." I always said this.

Eventually, B.J. figured this out. We're still friends, and she eventually left Y&R to help me when I became chief creative officer at McCann. She's had a very important creative director job at McCann since 1996. She is no longer a pushover, and although she still doesn't say no to unrealistic requests, now she makes sure everyone appreciates her efforts. B.J. is appreciated, *and* she has finally learned to be shrewd.

It was a good lesson to learn. If people want you to do something that you don't want to do, they have to know that it will be a sacrifice and a hardship. You don't want people *expecting* the above-and-beyond, because soon they will think it is their due. When that happens, you get "slave" status. It's a pit more women fall into than men, and once we're in that hole, it's hard to climb out. If you are a woman, I will bet money that you are far too accommodating.

"Snap out of it."*

Is It Luck, Great Timing, or Pure Genius?

Another lesson I learned along the road to the top is that timing is everything. I don't know how much of my success was calculated and how much was just the sheer good fortune of being in the right place at the right time, and frankly, it doesn't matter. Cer-

---

* Cher in *Moonstruck.*

tainly, it was a combination of the two, but one can never under-estimate the importance of a good three-way combo: luck, timing, and a great idea.

The first big blue-chip account I ever managed creatively was a disaster. I had just started working at McCann Erickson as a group creative director, and I was eager to make a mark on the presti-gious AT&T Business-to-Business account.

This client had never had a female creative director before, and I wanted to be the best creative leader they'd ever had. I thought that I would be successful because I loved technology, and the telecommunications business was hot at this time. Only three years earlier, AT&T had been a regulated monopoly. Then one day everything changed. On January 1, 1984, AT&T started the day as a new company. Of the $149.5 billion in assets it had the day be-fore, AT&T retained $34 billion. Of its 1,009,000 employees, it re-tained 373,000. The government had ended AT&T's monopoly and the company was never the same again. When I arrived on the scene, AT&T was deeply engaged in what was known as the "tele-phone wars." Upstarts like Sprint and MCI were battling AT&T for its residential and business-to-business turf. It was all very excit-ing to me, because in addition to technology, I love war games.

I had a vision for AT&T from the beginning. It was my belief that this big, monolithic giant needed to bring some humanity to its brand. Although the advertising to the residential customer was warm and fuzzy ("Reach out and touch someone"), the voice of AT&T to the business customer was the exact opposite. For some reason, AT&T must have believed that when people were in their office they were different than when they were in their homes, be-cause the advertising to the business customer was cold and effi-cient.

Three years after the monopoly ended, AT&T was still seen as arrogant. It was clear that the company had to get in touch with its female side, even though I didn't articulate it this way to our

AT&T clients. Whatever they heard me saying, they didn't agree. I had put my best creative people on the first assignment, but all of the ideas I presented fell on deaf ears.

After two months, I still hadn't sold any of the distinctive work we had created, and some of it had been perfect for them. It turned out that I wasn't being paranoid. I remember the meeting when they decided they had finally had enough of me. I had just shown them a charming but sophisticated animated campaign that explained a very complicated networking product that they offered to small companies. The campaign not only made the product desirable, but it presented AT&T as a human company that cared about its customers. At least, that's what I thought.

What the clients thought was that they needed a different creative director. I was asked off their business. They weren't even impressed that I actually *understood* how their damn network hierarchy platform worked. They just weren't buying *me*.

"What does this effete, Upper East Side, New York, *woman* know about the square-shouldered, Midwestern culture of AT&T?" one of the clients asked.

"I live on the Upper *West* Side," was my quick retort.

John Nieman, the executive creative director at McCann, New York, was firm in his support for me; in fact, he had hired me expressly to manage the AT&T business. To his credit, he refused to take me off the account, and after another painful month, AT&T decided to open up its business to other agencies. Three months on the account and the business was in review. I had the distinct suspicion that if I were a man, this would not have happened.

Our most senior account manager on the business, Hank O'Brien, was a soft-spoken former AT&T executive who was on the business at McCann because he understood AT&T's culture and because he had clout with the clients. Hank convinced the clients to give us one last chance before they talked to other shops. He promised that in two weeks (*"TWO WEEKS? Oh, GOD!"*), we would show them that we understood their brand, their complicated products, and how to reach their business customers. John Nieman was compelled to open the assignment up to other creative groups, because if we lost the AT&T business, there would be hell to pay. John Dooner (who was running New York and all of North America at the time) was personally involved, even though there were four other accounts in crisis on the exact same timetable. (For years following this, Dooner would brag about how we were in jeopardy on five critical pieces of business all at the same time, and how one by one, his five handpicked teams saved them all.)

But at the time I didn't know what to do, so I gathered a few creative people and headed over to AT&T's headquarters in Bedminster, New Jersey. When in doubt, talk to clients. It never hurts. Waiting for me there was a man named Joe. He turned out to be the Big Idea that would save the account, make me a hero, and change the face of AT&T.

This "Joe" I had discovered was Joseph Nacchio, the manager of AT&T's NOC center. NOC stands for Network Operations Center—the brains of AT&T. The NOC center included a huge board about fifty feet long and fifteen feet high that displayed news broadcasts, national weather patterns, maps of all the telephone routes throughout the United States, trouble areas, etc. It was a communications snapshot of the whole country.

Joe was young, confident, smart as a whip, and full of energy, and he was the first person I'd met at AT&T who made me think the company was dynamic. When he explained to me how fast AT&T could recover and reroute calls when a farmer's backhoe accidentally cut one of the company's cables, my heart went aflutter. I asked him to come to McCann's office and let me videotape him. My goal was to use him as the spokesman in a series of TV spots.

My account management partner was the young Eric Keshin, a big, burly, six-foot-four-inch alpha male as confident and smart as Joe was. The three of us would form a lasting partnership on the

AT&T business, but at the time, I didn't know Eric any better than I knew Joe. I was working on instinct alone. I never dreamed that this big lug would partner with me for the next twenty years and become the most important person in my career. All I knew was that Eric understood AT&T and the complicated telecommunications business, and I needed him.

So Joe came to McCann's office, and Eric and I asked him questions about the business that got him all riled up and those spirited answers made the best commercials. He was passionate and animated as he explained what AT&T did to make its network "robust," or self-healing, and how they could redirect calls instantaneously from one fiber-optic line to another after a cable was cut. He enthusiastically described how the company was competitive with new services for business customers and why AT&T was absolutely the best service provider that businesses could depend on. He was magnificent.

Eric and I talked to Joe for three hours, and I cut nine commercials. I edited the spots to appear as though we had just dropped in on Joe's conversation. Sometimes I started a spot in the middle of a sentence to give the feeling that the viewer just happened to be listening in. I wanted the commercials to feel real and in the moment, to give people a glimpse of the real AT&T and the people behind the curtain. I wanted viewers to share the enormous respect I had for the company and to believe that AT&T employed passionate, smart people their customers could trust and like.

I wanted the business customer to fall in love with AT&T. But even more, I wanted AT&T to be seen as a company people *wanted* to do business with.

On that frightening day when we presented all the work from the agency, I gathered the creative people together for a pep talk. We were on a combat mission, and I remembered a reassuring line from an old World War II movie. I used a version of it.

"We go in, we present, we get out," I said. "Nobody gets hurt."

In the movie, they weren't presenting creative ideas to AT&T, of course, they were merely going to blow up a bridge in Nazi territory swarming with enemy soldiers.

The meeting room was filled with the entire governing board of AT&T—twenty 800-pound gorillas who made all the decisions for what was arguably the most influential company in America at the time. One of them was the ferocious-looking CEO, who everyone said hadn't smiled since the divestiture of Ma Bell in 1984. I could see from just looking at him that this was probably true. It was intimidating to say the least, and he just glared at me. Between the AT&T board and the McCann team, I was the only woman in the room of thirty men.

The agency had prepared three campaigns to show these clients. The first two were painful to present. We had done traditional storyboards, and each thirty-second commercial had about five boards showing the pictures and copy that would deliver the message. To make things even more difficult, we had blown these boards up so that everyone could see them, but they were virtually impossible for one person to manage. The creative guy who presented this work, let's call him Lou, was a brilliant writer and a Rhodes scholar, but he appeared to have lost his mind right before he stood up to present. For some bizarre reason, Lou decided he would smoke a cigarette while he presented the work, and the combination of his cigarette ashes flying all over the place and those unwieldy boards made the presentation look like a skit from *Saturday Night Live.* Only no one was laughing. When Lou accidentally called an AT&T repairman a "pole climber"—the ultimate insult within AT&T culture—the room went dead silent, and Eric Keshin groaned. He did it quietly, almost to himself, but everyone heard it.

By the time it was my turn to present, our AT&T clients had been frowning through each and every one of the eight commercials that were presented in the first two campaigns. Our oversized storyboards littered their conference room, and the whole place looked like a graveyard for creative work. It actually *was* a cemetery, since everything was obviously dead and buried. All of the ashes from Lou's cigarettes added a nice touch.

Then it was my turn to stand up and face the group, like a mythical phoenix rising from those cigarette ashes, so to speak. I knew that if they saw my mind-numbing fear, I would be dead, too. I had to be tough, confident, authoritative, and a little arrogant. Exactly the opposite of what I was really feeling. But I had to be the "square-shouldered Midwestern *man*" their culture respected.

I walked to the front of the room without any storyboards, scripts, or even notes. All I had was a videotape in my hand, and in my head, a short but hard-hitting setup to the work I was about to show. In advertising, the setup is the positioning of what you are about to present. If it's done right, you can sell the work before you even show it. Conversely, a weak setup can damage even the most brilliant idea.

The first thing I told them was that the AT&T Business-to-Business brand had no personality. I thought this would get their attention—and it did. I said that the company was big and important, rich and powerful, but it had no soul. Being a monopoly from its inception had made it cocky and unapproachable.

"People don't trust you," I told these powerful men. "Your business customers are switching to an upstart competitor [MCI], even though the quality of their service isn't that good and their network is less reliable. And do you know why?"

Silence in the room.

"Because they *don't like you*." I heard John Dooner cough. Later, he told me that he wasn't worried, he was just gasping for air.

"And why is that?" I asked. "It's because they don't *know* you. And what makes that even worse is that your business customers *don't want to do business with you*."

It was harsh, but no one flinched. I was too nervous to be scared anyway. Sitting against the wall (we weren't allowed to sit at the conference table with the clients), John Dooner and Eric Keshin were now stone-faced. I looked at Eric and subtly raised one of my eyebrows. This was our code for "How am I doing?" He frowned and gave me a curt nod. I understood what a frown meant, and a nod was also clear, but the two of them together baffled me. I pressed on and ended my setup with as much male bravado as I could muster.

"But there is good news, gentlemen," I said. "We can change all that—*you* can change all that—with this."

I put my videotape in their machine and hit Play.

They watched my nine commercials with Joe Nacchio. He was energetic, informative, gutsy, and excited about his company. He was also happily enthusiastic about telecommunications and even made the business sound interesting. He exuded confidence and trust. You liked the guy and, in turn, he made you like AT&T. The nine spots all added up to an AT&T you wanted to do business with, a company that had the brains and the *passion* to do the right thing, the dedication to be the best on behalf of its customers, and the resources to make AT&T unquestionably The Right Choice.

Then I was supposed to ask if they had any questions, but I forgot. After the last commercial ended, I hit Stop, pulled out the cassette, and said, "Well, gentlemen, now what?"

Several of the men (*not* the CEO) had smiled during the presentation, and a few had even laughed while the more amusing spots were playing, but now there was dead silence in the room. Finally, the CEO spoke.

"I believe that Nina was lurking about at our staff meeting on Monday and heard every word we were saying."

Good God, it could so easily have gone the other way.

AT&T never reached out to other agencies, and we kept the business. The client who said I was an effete Upper East Side New

Yorker later bragged to everyone how I had captured the "voice of AT&T," and in time we even became good friends.

We ran those commercials and filmed additional dynamic AT&T people. The campaign did exactly as we had all hoped: It gave AT&T's business division a heart and a soul. AT&T had gotten in touch with its female side.

I was very fortunate that this turning point happened during my first six months as a group creative director at McCann. John Dooner, who went on to become the CEO of McCann Worldgroup, formed an opinion of me after that AT&T episode that has never changed. He had a cadre of home-run hitters in his mind, and I was now one of them. I had clout, and yet, it was still difficult for me to bask in this early glory.

There were only three people who worked on this account-saving campaign: Eric Keshin, Elaine Mixson, the producer who kept everything going, and me, the writer and creative director. It was my idea to use Joe, and I edited the spots. But Eric knew the right questions to ask, and between the two of us, we got great material. Eric basks in the glory of this achievement *to this day.* But at the time, when people praised me for saving the business, I was always speechless.

I believe it may have been the last time I was ever at a loss for words.

9

Reading Rooms and Other Handy Female Skills

How can you be successful in business if you can't read a room at a single glance? In any business where winning new clients is involved, there will be meetings with people you either don't know very well or don't know at all. These prospects may admire something about your company—otherwise they wouldn't be meeting with you—but they don't know who you are, and even more important, you don't know them. You are romancing strangers.

I don't know how you can win over someone you've never met without a keen ability to read a room and pick up tiny signals. And yet, most men don't have the antennae to do this. They might learn to do it, but it doesn't come naturally. That's why it's important to have women in the room. For boys clubs, the chances of having a high-ranking woman at a meet-and-greet is rare. For many years at McCann, I was usually the only senior woman in those meetings.

In advertising, as with most service businesses, we normally meet clients for the first time when we are trying to win their business. This first meeting is always a chemistry check. Clients are looking at us and other advertising agencies for one reason: They want to fall in love. It's astounding how many smart people in the advertising business don't understand this.

But even though new business prospects are looking for love, not everyone in the meeting will be in a receptive mood, at least, not at the beginning. In fact, in any given group, there will always be at least one or two people who may have a prejudice against your company and don't want to be in a meeting with you. You have to ferret out these people and win them over before they poison the whole group. This is especially tedious when one of these spoilers is also a top dog.

I have less of a problem when the top dogs are women. Women are easier to read than men. They are either going to admire me because I have also made it to the top of my company's ladder, and we will have an instant "Ya-Ya Sisterhood" thing going, or they will resent having another woman in the room and see me as competition. If that's the case, I'm happy to back off and let them bask in the spotlight alone.

While men might be a little harder to pinpoint, you can tell a lot about a man by learning to read the subtle signals he sends out. I used to be able to read a man instantly by the way he shook my hand. If he grabbed the tips of my fingers like I was a leper, he made it easy for me: I'd simply keep my mouth shut and see just how much resentment he harbored toward women and figure out whether it was all women or just me. Sometimes I was wrong about these men. They may have been uncomfortable with women, but it didn't necessarily mean that they feared or resented us. Regardless, these men could be won over.

Now, unfortunately, it's harder to read a man through a handshake. They're cheating. They're reading books, those little rascals. Now they *know* they're supposed to take a woman's entire hand comfortably and securely and look her right in the eye upon greeting. They practice this. It makes it harder to recognize a friend from a foe, but not impossible. It just means that while they are shaking your hand in this practiced, politically correct way, you have to draw them out. You can do this by testing what will make them laugh or at least smile at you with a quick Handshake Quip. This is a fast verbal jab while you have them in your grasp and they least expect it. It can take many forms. A veiled compliment usually works, like:

"*Nice tie.* Did *you* pick it out? No, wait. It was a gift, right?"

If he laughs, it tells me something: He's not too full of himself, he's not uptight, and he probably has good taste in ties, among other things. If he doesn't laugh, I learn even more. I am wary of a man who does not laugh easily and instinctively during a quick handshake with a woman. It could mean that he's wound up tighter than a drum. Under these circumstances, most people are anxious to find something to break the ice, and if they don't grab the chance, it means something is up. I am on guard with men like this.

Sometimes a little flirting works as a Handshake Quip.

"Your hands are cold," I'll say. "You know what Italian women say about a man with cold hands." He won't have the foggiest idea. "Cold hands, warm heart. True?" What man can resist such blatant flirtation? If he does resist, however, it tells me he'll be a tough nut to crack.

Here's the best Handshake Quip for when your tough nut is the CEO or someone who believes he is important:

"*I Googled you. Do you even* know *how many hits you have? Eight hundred and thirty-two.*"

The catch is that you *must* have Googled him. It's important not to bluff or lie when dealing with a man's ego.

After you soften up the room, the rest is easier. But be smart and get down to business quickly. You don't want men to think that you are the court jester and your only role is to loosen everyone up. You also have to be in a position of some authority for this to work.

Luckily, women read rooms subconsciously. Sometimes, we don't even know we are doing it. We just pick up signals, like magic. It's in our nature. Here's a classic scenario of this happening in a normal meeting:

Three men and two women have just returned from presenting new creative ideas to a very important client. They had all been working on this business for a year, and they knew the clients very well. They come into my office for a debriefing.

"How did the meeting go?" I ask. This one simple question is repeated millions of times every day in all companies, all industries, and all nations of the world. The only answer anyone ever wants to hear is "Great!" or a reasonable facsimile.

In this case, the three men oblige me:

"Great!" the first man says. "They want to proceed with everything."

"Test a few ideas, that sort of thing," the second says.

"All in all, a good meeting," the third man assures me.

"All in all, a good meeting" is male-speak for "nobody actually expired on the conference table."

I look at the two women, who were also there. They are not contributing anything to the assessment of the meeting. (The men outrank them.) I have to ask for their opinions.

"They hated everything," one of them says.

"They *said* that?" I ask. These particular clients are too notoriously repressed to be that open and honest with us, especially during a public meeting.

The other woman snorts. "Of course not. They're too repressed to be *honest* with us. But they never made *eye contact* with anyone. They sat back with their arms folded and glared at our collarbones. Ned [the senior client] kept sliding his chair away from the conference table. At one point we thought he'd just roll himself out the window."

"By the end, I think he wanted to *jump* out the window," the first woman says. "They said we could go on to testing . . . like if we had a *death* wish. *Could* go to testing, not *should*."

The men argue, pointing out specific things about the work that the clients liked. The women just shake their heads.

"You'd better call," the women say. "We are in deep doo-doo."

When I call Ned, I need a crowbar to pry the anxiety out of him. It becomes apparent that he has been upset for a while and no one noticed. When a client like this doesn't want to talk about a problem, it usually means that the relationship is so far gone, it's beyond discussion. It's clear, even over the phone, that this situation warrants a desperate measure. I listen to his concerns and guarantee him new work in three days.

We deliver on my promise, and everyone calms down. We had finally listened and reacted quickly. But what would have happened if I hadn't been alerted to the problem in time? We would have merrily tested work the clients didn't like, and we would have lost that account when it was so easy to fix the problem. And frankly, the problem should have been handled *in the meeting*. Why didn't this happen? There were several reasons.

First, two of the three senior men were creative people, and the third man was our most senior account manager. The "room readers" (the two women) were not senior enough to take control of the meeting. All they could do was watch the train wreck happen before their eyes. Shame on us for not having senior women on the business. Their intuition and perception would have made all the difference. And not just in that meeting, but in prior meetings that led us to this disastrous point.

Second, there were no "icebreakers" in the room—people who can use charm to break the tension when a meeting is going south.

The two young women noticed that the clients were upset, but they weren't skilled or confident enough to diffuse or de-escalate the clients' displeasure. So it just mounted. If someone had only said something funny, that could have opened the dialogue for a healthy discussion. If I had been there, I might have said, *"I can see by that scowl on your face that something is wrong here. Do you want to talk about it? Or should we just leave now so you can start drinking heavily?"*

Third, the women didn't even feel confident enough to discuss this problem with their male colleagues before they all got to my office. They must have known that the men were under the impression that the meeting went well. Why didn't they voice their concerns before they all came to me? Did the women feel that their opinions would fall on deaf ears? They shouldn't have waited to be asked for their impression of how the meeting went. They should have volunteered the information boldly and with conviction. What if the debriefing had been to a man instead of me? Would he have noticed a discrepancy within the team?

And what really happened in that client meeting? The three men were not idiots, but they took what the clients said at face value. They were listening with their ears and their *preconceived idea* of how they thought the meeting *should* go. They heard what their brains expected to hear. They were so confident that the agency was right, they didn't expect any other outcome, and after all, these clients did not give clear signals.

If the clients had said the work was "very creative," *every*one's antennae would have perked up. When clients say those two words, they are almost always being pejorative. "Very creative" is client-speak, and it means that the work is *too* creative. It will win creative awards (which few clients value), but it won't solve business problems.

But when clients say things like "interesting" and "we never thought of it this way"—two comments that can be sincere or not—at least we know that a little more information is needed to interpret what they mean correctly. This is where women have an advantage. We listen with our ears *and* our eyes.

At this meeting, the clients' body language was loud and clear, but only to the room readers. This is why it's so dangerous to have meetings without women in the room, or to have women who are there but afraid to trust their intuition and speak up. We have a different way of looking at things and a different set of tools for problem-solving. Our antennae are more sensitive than mens', and we can usually tell who our friends are and who wants us dead. Men tend to be oblivious to this. They can't imagine that anyone would want them dead.

Our ability to interpret verbal and nonverbal communication is a critical part of the natural gifts we bring to the table. When I was younger, I thought that I was just a gifted mind reader, but as I got more experience and worked with more and more intelligent women, I realized it was more of a gender thing. The only difference is that some women trust their instincts, while others are too insecure to listen to their own good judgment.

These instincts serve me well when I am doing the job most managers (and all creative directors) agree is the most difficult: hiring strangers. This is why we love to hire people we already know. It's not just because we like to hire our friends, we like to hire people we know we can trust.

The hardest jobs to fill are the managerial ones. How do you know what kind of leader a person will be? I get my best cues over food. I always take a managerial candidate out to breakfast or lunch to see how he or she treats the waitstaff. Without exception, the way this person treats our server will be the way he or she will treat the "little people" in the office. (I once had a candidate characterize employees as little people—I didn't hire him.) If the candidate is rude to the server or treats that person as though he or she is invisible, I don't want the candidate in my company. He or she will be a poor reflection on me.

Then there is the Six-Hour Plane Ride test. I got this idea from John Nieman. I would decide during an interview whether I could sit next to the candidate on a six-hour plane ride from New York to Los Angeles. If I didn't want to be with this person for that long, I could assume that no one else would want to either, and that solving problems with him or her would be painful. I always want to surround myself with talented people who are honest, decent, and fun to have in the room. Mary Ellen Cloyd, my insightful assistant and dearest friend for more than eighteen years, is a wise woman who would have made a brilliant leader. She always knew if I was going to hire someone by how long the interview lasted. A thirty-minute meeting could go either way, but if she had to come in and physically remove the candidate from my office because another meeting was scheduled to start, she knew the candidate was in like Flynn.

"You like this one," she would say with a glint in her eye.

Mary Ellen could read a room even when she wasn't *in* it.

———————

I spend a lot of time trying to get the alpha males of McCann in touch with some of the attributes that women have naturally. Sometimes they try. When Jim Heekin was CEO of McCann, he often tried to balance his macho male side with some female skills. One day he stopped by my office on his way back from a client meeting. He was so happy, I thought the meeting had been "Great!"

"It was a disaster," he said, grinning from ear to ear. "No one would look us in the eye," he continued cheerfully. "And they sat like this." He crossed his arms tightly in front of his chest and swiveled his chair around so that his back was almost facing me. Then he let out a huge bark of a laugh, slapped the table, and said, "I read the *room*!" He was so proud.

10

Are Men Braver than Women?

Are men programmed to be bigger risk-takers than women? Or are they just braver by nature? How much can we blame the customs and mores of our environment or our DNA? Can we blame our mothers, who raised us to be girly girls?

Do men actually *have* more courage, or are they just more reckless than we are? Maybe they are merely *acting* brave. Is there any real difference between actual bravery and bravado?

For the last half of my life, I have pretended to be brave many more times than I actually *was* brave. I am still hoping it will be a self-fulfilling prophecy.

Bloody, Bloody Coke (2002)

For years I had a recurring nightmare. I'm walking down a street, minding my own business, when suddenly, out of nowhere, a big red Coca-Cola delivery truck comes barreling down the street, aiming right at me. I try to dodge out of the way, but the truck is as nimble as I am. I move to the left, and the truck moves to the left; I dodge to the right, and the truck follows. It gets closer and closer and I begin to run out of steam. Finally, the truck hits me. The rest of the dream is a bird's-eye view of the accident scene; it's almost as if I am hovering over the carnage. All I see is a lot of blood. And it's all mine.

In 2002, my dream sort of came true. After losing the Coke business ten years earlier, McCann was finally getting another crack at this beloved brand, and as chief creative officer of the New York office, I was leading the charge. We'd been working on Coca-Cola for a few weeks. My very best creative people were working exclusively on breakthrough ideas so we could knock the socks off these new clients.

Our first big meeting was at Coke's headquarters in Atlanta, Georgia. We arrived armed with twenty television commercials and four original songs. We were going to wow them with the scope of our brilliance and our uncanny understanding of the Coca-Cola brand. After all, no one had worked on Coke longer than McCann Erickson had, and no one loved the brand more than we did.

The meeting consisted of eight McCann people and fourteen Coke clients. We all filed into a large boardroom, where a sumptuous lunch had just been enjoyed—by the clients, not us. After some pleasantries ("Hey, what about those *Braves!*"), I stood at the head of the table to set up our work. As soon as I was on my feet I got a nosebleed.

This was not a dainty, feminine little drizzle. No. It was a gusher. It was as if there were a pulmonary artery in my nose that had been severed. Blood was *pouring* out of my nose like water from a hose, and there was no way to stop it. I tried to pretend it wasn't happening and kept talking, holding my nose with tissues that quickly soaked. I didn't want to be seen as a wimp.

The Coke clients, a decent group of men, were horrified. They kept handing me the large white cloth napkins from their lunch that were scattered around the table and asking if I wanted to take a break, but I refused.

I had become philosophically opposed to taking breaks. Just a year before, a "break" precipitated losing a $350 million business. We were showing our irreverent Gateway Computers clients a new round of creative work, and halfway through the presentation, I asked if they wanted to take a "nature" break. They left the room and never came back. After waiting for almost an hour, I went looking for them, and I found them sitting in the CEO's office, smoking cigarettes and staring out the window.

"What are you *doing* here?" I asked them.

"Smoking."

They offered me a cigarette. I had stopped smoking twelve years earlier, but I took the cigarette. They seemed to be staring at something interesting outside the large window, but I knew for a fact that there wasn't anything interesting in their entire town. As they often said themselves, they were located in the armpit of America.*

The cigarette tasted awful. Why was I smoking again?

"Are you coming back to the meeting?" I asked them.

They didn't think so.

"We have more ideas to show you," I said. "You don't want to see them?"

They nodded.

"You *do* want to see them?"

"No."

Then I snapped.

"Well, you could have said so an hour ago. We could have gotten an earlier flight out of this hellhole."

There's a difference between acting brave and being reckless, a

---

* This was before they moved to their current headquarters in Irvine, California. Definitely not an armpit.

distinction I had not perfected at the time. I went back to the meeting room and told my team that the clients weren't coming back. We gathered up all of our work and headed out to the large van we had rented, because it was a *two-hour* drive to civilization and the nearest airport.

"They're going to fire us," one of the young account managers said.

Everyone looked at him with disgust. No shit. Of course they were going to fire us. We pulled into a convenience store to buy beer and salty snacks. This combo idea was Eric Keshin's big insight from his college days: The salt helps you retain the liquid, so you don't have to go to the bathroom so often. You just get bloated. Eric was brilliant like that.

"Maybe they *won't* fire us," Eric said as we headed out. "Oh, wait a second," he added sarcastically. "Our chairman called their corporate headquarters a shit hole. We're dead."

"*Hell*hole," I said. "I would never say 'shit' to a client."

We got our beer and salty snacks at a seedy convenience store, and I also bought bread, cold cuts, and mustard so I could make sandwiches for everyone during the two-hour ride to the airport. I had a need to nurture.

The Gateway story ended badly. After building up their business for three years and quadrupling their stock value with our aggressive, sales-producing retail strategy, we were fired soon after. In an e-mail.

The news traveled fast throughout McCann New York. Back at the office, Eric and I were sulking in the hallway when we ran into our boss, John Dooner. He called us into his office.

"So, you lost Gateway," he said, as if we needed to be reminded.

"Yeah," I said. "Win some, lose some." I could say this because we mostly *won* business for that New York office, and Eric and I had surplus clout. It's one of the reasons I was made chairman.

"She told them their corporate headquarters was a shit hole," Eric told Dooner.

"Did you really say that?"

"No. *No.* I did *not* say that. I would never say 'shit' to a client."

It was to Dooner's credit that he was taking this so well. Gateway brought in a lot of revenue. It helped our cause that we had won an unprecedented number of new business pitches over the past several years, and that the $350 million Gateway business, although significant, would be replaced soon enough. John Dooner knew that. Still, most CEOs would have called their senior managers on the carpet for losing such a big account. But all Dooner really wanted to know was how confident we were in the face of the loss.

"So what happened?"

"They took a break to go to the bathroom, and they never came back to the meeting," I said.

"Shit," Dooner said.

"Exactly," I said.

Eric wasn't saying much of anything. He was really angry about the whole thing. He'd invested a lot of his time and emotions into making the Gateway business take off, and he had created a retail/advertising model that drove their business through the roof.

"What does this do to your numbers?" John asked us. We always made our numbers at the end of the year. Eric made that happen. A few years later, John would make him chief operating officer for McCann Worldgroup.

Eric shrugged. "We'll be okay."

And we were okay, but you can see why I became sensitive about letting clients out of my sight when we were presenting to them.

So no breaks were even considered during that bloody Coke meeting. I would tough it out. Thank God the clients had just been eating lunch in our meeting room. They had an unending supply of cloth napkins, and my blood soaked through every one of them. When I finished the setup, our creative people presented all the work, but I don't think they had the clients' undivided attention. All eyes kept darting over to me to watch the progress of my terminal nosebleed.

As soon as the last song was played and the last TV idea was presented and the last client comment was made, my nose stopped bleeding. We packed up all of our stuff, and when we left it looked like an elephant had bled to death on the conference room table.

We didn't sell any of our creative work that day. I bled for nothing. And what did I prove? I was trying to be brave. Trying to tough it out. Trying to act like a man. If I let a little blood deter me from my mission, what would that have said about me? I didn't want anyone to know that I was scared to death we would lose the Coke business again—and this time on my watch.

What Is Courage Anyway?

In order to be heroic, shouldn't you be afraid of an outcome? Or as John Wayne said, "Courage is being scared to death but saddling up anyway." People who are unafraid aren't nearly as brave as the ones who know they will die and still rush headlong into battle.

In general, I found that while the alpha men of McCann were fearless, the alpha women were more courageous. A good example of this occurred in 2000. We were looking for a big retail account to soothe our ruffled feathers after losing a pitch for JCPenney. The opportunity came along in the form of a petite, attractive blonde named Julie Gardner. At the time, Julie was the senior vice president of marketing at Kohl's.* She was looking for a new agency to

---

* Currently, Julie is EVP, chief marketing officer at Kohl's.

handle their wildly successful and growing network of stores. But she didn't want to do a formal review. She believed that in choosing an advertising agency, relationships were equally as important as resources, and she thought it was a better use of her time to just meet with the contenders for her business to see if she liked and trusted any of us.

"I wanted to focus on talent and chemistry, and get a good cultural match," she told me recently. "As opposed to a long, drawn-out dog-and-pony show that would be meaningless and require a lot of unnecessary resources on everyone's behalf." (You can see why we loved her from the beginning.)

She was right. A formal review can take up to three months, and even then a client doesn't always get the right people for the job.

So Julie chose four or five agencies based on the quality of work that was being done for existing clients and their ability to handle an account as large as Kohl's. Then she scheduled time for her and a few of her staff members to visit all the agencies. She gave us each six hours, and we could use that time any way we wanted.

Eric Keshin had a brilliant idea. He believed that we could win Julie over by demonstrating our quick problem-solving ability and grace under pressure—two strengths that were vital for succeeding on retail accounts. His plan was to offer Julie an "ad in a day." He would ask her to give us an assignment as soon as she arrived, and we would demonstrate our fast, shoot-from-the-hip thinking by solving the problem strategically and creatively before she left. That meant in six hours, we would have to create a strategy (the normal time for this is two weeks), think of a creative idea (normally another two weeks), and do a storyboard (if we pay illustrators overtime, we can do it in twenty-four hours). There was no way we could do any of this in just six hours.

The two other men in the room were the codirectors of strategic planning, Nat Puccio and Suresh Nair. They agreed with Eric and thought this was a brilliant idea. Besides myself, there were two women in the room: Marjorie Altschuler, our brilliant but apprehensive director of new business, and Joyce King Thomas, our rising star and my strong number two. They were as horrified as I was. As creative people, Joyce and I were afraid that this would devalue the creative process. First, we calmly stated our feelings, saying it was risky and unnecessary, but we couldn't budge Eric. Finally, our fears (and I like to believe our common sense) took control of the situation, and we became more emphatic.

"ARE YOU NUTS?" I said. "This will be *shit*. Maybe we can figure out a *strategy* in six hours, but we could never do a TV spot. And why do we want them to think we can work this fast anyway? How will they respect the creative process after this? What will they expect if we get their business? *'Ads While U Frigging Wait?'* "

Our final words on the subject were emphatic and intractable. *"THIS IS TOTALLY UNACCEPTABLE!"*

But in the end we all agreed to Eric's Big Idea. The women were terrified of failing, but we agreed to it anyway. The men just assumed we could pull it off, confident for no apparent reason.

So Julie Gardner and her team walked into our large conference room that fateful day, and she gave us a problem: low store traffic in Dallas and two other key cities. How could we increase customer visits? We came up with a strategy based on the company's unique business position: Kohl's carries all of the current top brands, with a deep inventory of styles, colors, and sizes, at ridiculously low prices. It's the ideal place to shop when you have kids and they keep growing (a direct consequence of feeding them several times each and every day).

It took us less than an hour to come up with our strategy, thanks to our strong insight, which is always the key to a fast and brilliant solution. I had just taken my three strapping teenage nephews to Kohl's the week before, and because the prices were so good, I let them buy whatever they wanted (and there was a lot for them to want). It was refreshing to be able to say yes to everything without worrying about the cost. And that led to the idea of "A Yes Culture." When you come to Kohl's, you can find everything that you're looking for at such a good value that you don't have to say no. Julie loved it. (She still reminds me of this strategy today.)

The creative execution was simple and adorable. We didn't have time to get pictures drawn, so we used existing film to make a "rip," which is short for rip-off. This is a simulated spot that can never run on air because it contains footage from existing sources like movies and other commercials. Then we edit it with music and our own copy. It gives a client a good sense of what the final commercial will feel like.

This spot opened with tight close-ups of the most adorable children on earth, from the ages of a few months old to six or seven years old. As their faces appear one after the other, we hear a great music track and the distinctively warm voice of the copywriter, who wrote the spot and was also an actress. As one beautiful little face fades into another, we hear her say: "Yes. Yes. Yes. How can you say no to this? When you come to Kohl's, you never have to say no." Then we show all the great name-brand items for kids at ridiculously low prices and end by saying, "Every day there's always something new at Kohl's, at prices you don't have to resist. Kohl's, where the answer is always yes." We ended the commercial with that line under their logo:

Kohl's.

The Answer Is Always Yes.

A week later, Kohl's gave us all of their business. Julie said that all of the agencies were good, but we were the one she trusted. She believed we would get her to the next level. And we have never let her down.

Later, Eric reminded me that he never promised a "finished" spot to Kohl's; that was my idea. He also wanted to know if I was going to fudge this story in this book so that he would come off looking bad, but I admit that he has always had more courage than I had. I like to think it was because I had the responsibility of the creative product on my shoulders, and that if I failed, my humiliation would be much more public than his, but I'm not sure that this was the entire reason. Eric admitted that he was a little nervous, too, but *it didn't stop him.* He likes to say that he had total confidence in our ability as a team to pull off the instant solution, but it was a leap of faith for him at the time. I just know it.

And that brings me back to my bravery theory: Maybe men don't have more courage than we do. Maybe they *just act like they do.* Is this possible? Can we pretend to be fearless and eventually *be* fearless? Is it a self-fulfilling prophecy? I think so. We just need to keep taking chances. Small ones at first, and when we see that we don't die, we can take bigger ones. But how do we begin?

Can We Fake Confidence?

Isn't this what bravado is? Faking courage? As I was learning to be more like the men I worked with, I started to take even greater risks. But acting brave is harder than it sounds.

It's a knee-jerk reaction to panic in the face of danger. We're only human, and often panic *does* seem like the smartest course of action. That's why we have adrenaline. But when we fake confidence, we have to behave abnormally. It's not very different from controlling a spooked horse.

When something terrifies your horse, he wants to take off and get the hell out of danger. He will panic and become hysterical, jumping, turning, and whinnying, and you're not sure if he will just take off and get the two of you to safety. You don't want him in charge, because he may no longer notice nor even care that you're still on his back. Your knee-jerk reaction is to pull in the reins, clamp your knees tighter around his body, and lean forward, just in case you have to cling on to his neck for dear life and yell into his ear to *stop. But this is all wrong.* You're supposed to do just the opposite. In the midst of utter and complete fear and panic, you have to act counterintuitively and *loosen* your knee grip so that the horse feels you relax. (How ridiculous is that?) You should never loosen the reins completely, but don't pull back on them either. Sit up straight, balance your butt on the saddle, and lean *back.* Then talk to him calmly and gently so that you soothe the panic out of him. And you have to do all of this when every fiber of your being screams for you to grab that horse's neck and hang on tight. But the most important thing is to *relax* so the horse thinks that you are not scared, and you can get him out of the mess he thinks the two of you are in.

The same technique works at the office.

At McCann—as at all high-pressure businesses—we develop little ploys for keeping our panic under wraps until our brains kick in and we're able to solve the problem. Mine is the "so what" trick, and I use it when someone tells me something so horrible, my brain turns to mush. I can *think* whatever I like, but whatever I *say* is preceded by "So what!"

A colleague might say:

"*OHMYGOD. We lost the global Motorola business to Ogilvy.* [A loss of $200 million in billing and $15 million to $20 million in revenue.] *We are dead! AUUUGGGHHHHH!*"

I might be thinking:

Holy crap. This is worse than dying. This is just plain humiliating.

But I would calmly say out loud:

"*So what!* We can replace two hundred million dollars in three months."

Or someone would tell me:

"*OHMYGOD. The client just killed our campaign, and he expects to see something totally new by Monday. And today is FRIDAY. AUU-UGGGHHHHH!*"

I might be thinking:

Crap, crap, crap. We'll never think of anything good enough by then.

But I would calmly say out loud:

"So what! This is why God invented weekends. We'll have something great in two days."

In both cases, I'm not diminishing the significance of our problems; I just know that we need confidence to dig ourselves out of the holes we're in. The real disaster is for us to believe we're losers.

Act brave and you will look brave.

Perception *is* reality.

Simulated courage is a good weapon to keep in your arsenal. It's handy in business and all other facets of your life.

3

THE AIR IS THIN
AT THE TOP

Do some soul-searching. How badly do you want to get to the top in a boys club? And when you get there, how badly will you want to stay there? What will you forfeit along the way for the sake of success? For power? What will you sacrifice for the people who work for you? If it becomes necessary to bend the truth to protect them, could you do it? Would you sacrifice a few people for the good of the majority? Would you do just about anything (legal) to win? Most men will do all of this and more. But do *you* have the stomach for it?

If your aim is to get to the top through the Plexiglas barrier, these are the questions that need to be answered before you give up too much to get there. And make no mistake about it; you will have to make sacrifices. More than you ever dreamed possible.

Everything I learned during the first eighteen years of my advertising career was preparation for the job I always coveted: running the creative department of a big, important New York advertising agency. To my knowledge, no other woman had ever held this position.

When I finally got my big break, it wasn't anything like what I had imagined. I never dreamed that after struggling so hard to get the job, I would have to fight even harder to keep it.

This is a painful lesson for anyone to learn, but it is even more difficult for women. It's almost as if we use all of our energy and talent to get to the top of the mountain, and then we run out of psychological steam once we get there.

Just remember that it's dangerous at the top of that ladder. It's wobbly, you're all alone, and the air is so thin, you almost can't breathe.

But if you can make it and learn to take deep breaths, the rewards for leading a boys club are huge and like nothing you've ever experienced before.

And it can be a lot of fun. If you can just manage to stay alive.

11

How to Outmaneuver Men Who Outrank You

Sometimes we want to climb a mountain just because it's there and we believe we can make it to the peak without killing ourselves. But there is always a price to pay for sitting on top of the world. Always. It will be your health, your happiness, your kids, your marriage, or if not any of those, your peace of mind, and maybe even a piece of your integrity. Sometimes you may even have to violate your own personal code to get there. You need to think about these things before you race off for the summit.

For instance, while you are climbing your way to the top, what do you do when you find yourself working for a bad man? It's bound to happen. How do you handle someone you don't respect or trust or even like? What if he is a danger to the rest of the office, and no one is in a position to stop him? What if he is not *worth* the effort of seduction and manipulation? I have only one piece of advice under these circumstances: Find another job.

And yet, what if the situation is not so black-and-white? The annoying thing about human beings is our pesky shades of gray, which make clear-cut decisions so difficult. What if your boss is also very smart? What if he is bipolar and only mean half the time? Can you deal with guessing which one of his multiple personalities will show up to the office every day? Does his good side outweigh the pain caused by his dark side? If you are powerless to do anything about a person like this, and if working for him makes you sad to be alive, then you should find another boss. Life is too short to suffer fools or bastards. But what if your biggest problem is not your boss at all, but someone else on the food chain who totally outranks you and has the power to make your life a living hell?

What do you do then?

And what if you are in a position to change the status quo? Then what?

Think Before You Leap

It's always a good idea to talk over big decisions with someone, such as a colleague or partner who has your best interests at heart and can put things in perspective. But sometimes you want something so badly, you won't listen to anyone, or even your own good instincts.

It would be more rewarding for me if I could rewrite history here and say that I always did my homework before accepting a job, but when I took the top creative job at McCann Erickson, I ignored all of the warning signs that hinted at disaster. I thought I was returning to a place that was very familiar to me, because I had once known the culture and all of the key players. But the culture had shifted when I left McCann in 1991 to join JWT, and the new key players were virtual strangers to me. This became apparent before I committed to the job, but I didn't think it was important.

The first warning sign came before I even negotiated my contract. My husband and I had flown to New York to meet with the two men who were to be my "partners," Peter Kim and Jim

Heekin. I had known them both when we were all at J. Walter Thompson (they were the driving forces at the JWT New York office while I was the creative director for JWT/Chicago). McCann hired Peter in September 1993 as vice chairman of Worldgroup and chief strategy officer. Jim was hired at around the same time to be regional director of North America, and it was clear that he was a candidate for the top job as CEO John Dooner's replacement— not right away, but in time.

My husband and I were scheduled to meet them and their wives for a pleasant dinner. It was an attempt on Dooner's part to have us work as a team from the beginning. We were meant to bond.

But when we got to the restaurant, only Jim and Peter were there, and it was obvious that they had been waiting for us for a while. Peter appeared to have been drinking—at least, that was what I hoped at the time, because a totally different person had replaced the quiet wunderkind I had known at JWT. This Peter Kim was unrecognizable to me. He kept talking loudly, telling me that the three of us had to do battle at McCann. We had to *destroy* everyone who opposed his master plan.

"We will kill them," he kept saying. *"Dead, dead, dead."*

He punctuated each "kill" or "dead" by making karate chops in the air, and then he'd slam his hand on the table for emphasis. All of the tableware went flying every time he slammed his hand down, and soon the people at the surrounding tables stopped talking to one another and stared at us. Brian and I were in shock. Thankfully, after almost half an hour of this aggressive behavior, the proprietor of the restaurant came to our rescue. He kicked us out. He told us that we were disturbing the other guests, and we were asked to leave.

Peter had so stunned my husband that, on the way back to our hotel, he just assumed that I would never join a company that would employ someone like the Peter Kim we had just left. Years later, Brian would say that two things changed his mind: The first thing happened the very next night. We had dinner with John Dooner, and Brian left that dinner understanding why I trusted and cared for John so much. The second thing was something I'd said to Brian after we left Jim and Peter at that restaurant, when Brian was determined to save me from myself and take me back to Chicago.

"Don't worry," I'd said. "Peter won't be here in twelve months."

It wasn't that I was out to get Peter. What I meant was that I knew McCann's culture (surprisingly good-hearted for a boys club) and it would never allow someone like Peter to last very long. I knew that Peter would either temper his ways or be forced out.

So I took the job. But even with that first meeting emblazoned on my mind, I was totally unprepared for what I found when I returned to the familiar office of my alma mater. What's more, for the first time in my career, I was partnered with a man I didn't want to seduce and couldn't imagine how to manipulate. I was in a total mess from the moment I walked through the doors on November 9, 1994, as the first female EVP, executive creative director, of McCann/New York. During the three years I was gone, a whole new agency had been formed, and it was not a pretty sight. If J. Walter Thompson/Chicago was a dangerous job in 1991, McCann in 1994 was Armageddon. It even looked like a war zone, and people were leaving in droves—good people, the ones you don't want to lose. This exodus had been going on for two years, and on my first day, there were three farewell parties planned for the latest defectors from the creative department.

Part of the problem was Coke-related. While I was in Chicago, the brand that had defined McCann's creative reputation for decades had left. Coca-Cola had fired McCann in North America, and we were no longer known as "the Coke agency." Who were we now? The agency was dead in the water with no momentum, and we were totally schizophrenic. We had become a house divided, and even worse, an armed camp. It was Jim and Peter against the rest of McCann, which included a small but vocal group that was out to get these two men fired. This group believed that Jim and Peter still harbored the deep-seated prejudice that J. Walter Thompson felt toward McCann. JWT people had always referred to McCann as a company of "ad thugs" and said the agency was in the business of making margins, not advertising. McCann people thought JWT had no backbone. Nice way to begin a relationship.

On my first day back, Marjorie Altschuler came to my office in hysterics. Jim had hired this five-foot-tall, ninety-pound dynamo to be the director of new business. She was an uncompromising whirlwind of energy and anxiety. The fact that I grew to adore her is an indication of how much her innate goodness and talent outweighed her impossible angst. Over the years, we turned her name into a verb. We would say, "We've been Marjied." It meant that she had totally worn us down, and now we were doing whatever she wanted us to do. It was a tactic that worked for her. To this day I am crazy about the woman, but during my first meeting with her, I did not envision a long-lasting friendship.

She came to my office carrying two shopping bags filled with videotapes. She was disgusted and angry.

"I can't put a creative reel together for a new business pitch," she said, calmly at first. Then, less calmly: "I CAN'T PUT A FRIGGING REEL TOGETHER."

"That's ridiculous," I said. Showing a prospect the agency's creative reel is critical for new business, and without a good reel of our best, most *recent* work, we don't stand a chance at being included in any new-business review.

"I need ten good spots," Marjie said, practically in tears, and she dumped the shopping bags on my desk. They were filled with the last twelve months of TV production. "Find me three I can use and you'll be a genius."

I spent all night looking at the agency's TV commercials. Since I could only include work from existing clients, I had to eliminate our best work on Coke. I found one good commercial, a recent AT&T spot that was produced brilliantly. I cheated and added another spot that I loved, even though it was almost three years old. The spot was cute as hell, and it always put everyone in a good, receptive mood for the rest of the reel.

It opened with a little shar-pei puppy totally enveloped in those characteristic folds. He is sitting on a pillow, minding his own business. As an announcer voice-over introduces a new Black & Decker steam iron, the screen fills with steam. Then the voice says that this iron has so much steam, it gets out even the toughest wrinkles. As the steam clears, we see the baby shar-pei with wrinkle-free skin. Puppies and kids. Always works. I opened every reel with this spot for two years before I had something better. The first time I showed the agency reel at a new-business meeting without that shar-pei commercial, everyone in the meeting applauded. It meant we had finally stopped living in the past.

But on my first day on the job, we had a new-business reel with two commercials on it. Not an encouraging beginning. I thought about other ways we could win over a prospect. Maybe we could use our charm. But did we even have any of that? It didn't appear to me that anyone here even liked one another; how could we be charming together?

After my first week, I was officially stunned. How did McCann get to this sorry state?

For one thing, the office hadn't had a full-time creative director for two years. McCann Worldgroup's vice chairman and world-wide creative director Marcio Moreira would have been a great candidate for the New York job if he'd wanted a demotion, and he did try to keep the New York plates spinning. But he literally had the world on his shoulders and was constantly on a plane to put out fires halfway around the globe.

Marcio needed a solid creative director for New York, but after Coke left, the job lost its luster, and star creative talent didn't want any part of the *ex*-Coke agency. I didn't know which was lower, our creative reputation or the morale of the office. And the word on the street was not helpful to our self-esteem.

"Does your wife know what she's getting into at McCann?"

My husband, who is also in the advertising business and was interviewing for a New York position at the time, would hear this warning from every recruiter he met.

"We've been trying to fill that creative director slot for two years. No one wants it. Does your wife *know* what she's getting into?"

"It's the most dangerous job in New York right now."

"The place is a hellhole. No one wants to work there."

"Does your wife know what she's getting into?"

I thought that I did. I promised my husband that McCann was most assuredly *not* a hellhole. Marcio, John Dooner, and Eric Keshin were there, and I trusted these three men. I also thought I knew why they wanted me back, other than the distinct possibility that no one else wanted the job.

First of all, I was a known entity to both Dooner and Jim Heekin. Dooner saw me as a McCann person (he always referred to my three years in Chicago as a "sabbatical"). And Heekin saw me as a JWT person after watching Steve Davis and me revitalize the Chicago office. They hoped I could bridge the gap between those vastly different cultures and bring the two warring groups together. By 1994, the gulf was already wide and getting wider every day.

The second reason is the one I love the most: McCann needed some alpha females. A high-ranking woman on the board of directors of a big, global McCann client had told John Dooner that he needed "a few good women at the top of his boys club."

The third reason is that Dooner loved me. Always did. Always will. He knew I was one more person he could trust without question.

My first order of the day was to wrest control away from the person who had been playing creative director before I came and still thought he was more qualified for the job than I was. I had to outmaneuver Peter Kim, a man who not only outranked me (like Marcio, he was vice chairman of the entire Worldgroup organization, not just New York), but who was also a master Machiavellian tactician. He kept an ancient Chinese sword in his office, and his bible was *The Art of War* by Sun Tzu. He carried it around with him all the time. The book, not the sword. Well, sometimes the sword.

As vice chairman and chief strategy officer of Worldgroup, Peter was one of the most powerful men in the entire global network of McCann Erickson. He had been brought in as an "agent of change" and was given carte blanche to do whatever was needed to improve the creative reputation of the agency. During the fourteen months he was there without a full-time and dedicated creative director onboard, his primary focus was to win back the coveted Coca-Cola account, but having failed at that, he now turned his attention toward building his power base.

Under the circumstances, it was easy to see why Peter believed that *he* was the real creative leader of the agency and naturally assumed that he wielded enough power to override the authority of a newcomer, not to mention a mere woman. I knew that because I had earned a reputation in Chicago for being a nurturing and collaborative leader, he thought I would be a pushover. While this was a big mistake, an even bigger error in his judgment was his conviction that he could control the creative product of the agency once I was there. This was an untenable situation that had to be corrected quickly. But as problems go, it was just a drop in the bucket. First, I had to survive the first six months of the worst year of my life.

As a woman, and one who had never had to confront a man like this before, I was not prepared or trained to do battle with some-one like Peter. And yet, the people who will threaten us the most when we reach these high levels are going to be men like him. When we get to the top, we need even stronger powers of seduc-tion and manipulation, and we need something else: the ability to fight with these men on their own terms and act more like them than is comfortable for us. But you can't seduce and/or manipulate the Big Boys if you're squeamish.

When you play for such high stakes, the need to understand your adversaries takes on a whole new meaning. It is one thing to seduce and manipulate the men who work alongside you or for you; it is a whole new ball game to control men who outrank you. This is especially true if you don't report to them, because then they have no reason to mentor or support *you*. They didn't hire you or even inherit you. You are not *their* person. In Chicago, the men who initially resented me did not outrank me. I used seduc-tion and manipulation to win them over because I needed them and there were just too many of them to eliminate without deci-mating the agency. McCann's New York office was different. I had a lot of support from below. It was the people at the top that had me worried.

As a woman, your instincts will always be very valuable to you, and you will probably be able to identify those who don't support you fairly quickly, but when you are at the top of an organization, you have to be sure who your enemies are beyond a shadow of a doubt. I have seen women fail at these top jobs, and when the backstory is revealed, it is almost always because they didn't use their instincts or their feminine skills to *read the damn room*. They didn't recognize the culture or how dangerous their adversaries re-ally were. As we get to these positions of power and influence, we run the risk of becoming as arrogant as the men. Don't let that happen to you. Don't believe your own press, watch your back, and don't take anything for granted.

Respect Your Adversary's Power

Make a good assessment of your opponent's power in the company. Is it real or imagined? Whose ear does he have? How much damage can he do to you? Tread gently and slowly while you accumulate this information. If you start swinging right out of the gate, you'll have nowhere to go when you want to up the ante. So begin by asserting yourself quietly. You never know, subtlety could work. Peter was way too important to take down in one round anyway. It was far easier to try to win him over than to get rid of him. Plus, he was smart. The agency needed him. Hell, *I* needed him.

Although I was aware of Peter Kim's disrespect for almost everyone at McCann, I had to give him a chance to interact directly with me. After the restaurant episode, my next inkling that this man was trouble happened during my first week on the job, when he unveiled his Great Creative Plan to me. He came to my office with exciting news.

"We need to break new ground," he said to me. "Operate in ways no other agency would dare to attempt. We have to be bold and fearless."

Only a fool would disagree with that logic.

"I was thinking how powerful and *newsworthy* it would be," he said, "to have guest creative directors onboard." Peter loved to get press for the agency—as well as for himself. He lived for it.

"What do you mean?" I asked, eyeing all of the boxes in my office that I still hadn't unpacked.

"Guest creative directors," he repeated. "We would bring them in for new-business pitches on a freelance basis, handpicking the ones most skilled at whatever business we're going after. It's brilliant, don't you think?"

Forget how insulting this was to me. It was impractical. If we won a pitch with a freelance creative director, the clients would expect this person to run their business, or at least have some impact on it. If this person didn't actually work for us, it would be a problem. This was clearly a plan that wasn't worked out very well.

Then Peter unfolded a list of hotshot creative directors, most of whom had been fired from their creative director responsibilities because they couldn't win new business.

I thought about the best way to answer Peter, something emphatic and diplomatic that would get us off to the right start with each other. Something like:

"Hell, NO!"

I hadn't even finished unpacking yet and he was already sure that I couldn't do the job. I told him that I was the creative director of the New York office, and that I would be running all of the new-business pitches as well as making all of the creative decisions for the office. This was not negotiable, I told him. It appeared that he accepted my stake in the ground, because he didn't have a rebuttal. But remember your training with men: It's not what you *say* that's important; it's what they *hear.* God only knows what Peter was hearing. He dropped his guest-creative-director plan and later found other ways to outmaneuver me. It was clear that he still thought of himself as the creative and spiritual leader of the agency, and I needed to prove to the rest of the office that I was the better "man" for the job.

It is very dangerous to butt horns with a high-ranking officer of a company, especially if you're a woman. You must be sure that you have enough clout to protect yourself and that you have the guts to use it when the need arises. Then you must be absolutely sure that this person is beyond redemption. *Don't make it personal.* You could wind up sacrificing a key member of the company just because you listened to venom from others or because you simply disliked the person.

When you are holding the reins, however, you don't have the luxury of acting on your emotions. You have a company to consider. But take notes. Keep a diary of grievances with the date and time, just in case you need it one day. You should also be sure that you're doing the right thing, and that your actions are for the benefit of the whole organization. I had to be sure that the vice chairman of McCann Worldgroup was a true danger to the New York office and not just to me. It was a hard discipline to accept, but it was the right thing to do, even though every fiber in my being just wanted him to go away.

To make matters worse, there were shades of gray with Peter. The young man I had known at JWT was smart and clever. At McCann, however, while he was still young at thirty-five and rocket-scientist smart, he had become a dictator. Within the first few months of our relationship, I suspected that the problems with Peter were not controllable or fixable. It was simply in his nature to be impatient, rude, and arrogant, the emotional hat trick often attributed to geniuses. He just might have been too smart to lead in a business where collaboration is key.

There were a lot of straws that led to finally breaking my camel-like back during our first year together. My unusually high tolerance for unruly "stars"—which I developed by running creative departments—was even higher for Peter Kim, but in the end it was clear that one of us would have to go.

Our relationship was a disaster from the beginning. At the end of my first week on the job, I attended a new-business pitch to AT&T for an additional part of its business. We still had the business division, but we wanted more. Since I'd had a strong relationship with the AT&T clients in the past, I was asked to attend this meeting even though I hadn't supervised the creative ideas.

When we got to the clients' conference room in New Jersey, it was discovered that unbeknownst to anyone, Peter had invited another company to participate in the pitch. While we were setting up for the presentation, two nice young men—another creative resource, we were told later—were being introduced to everyone. They even had twenty minutes on an already crowded agenda to present their ideas—which no one other than Peter had seen before. Not the group creative director who had done all of the work for McCann, not even Eric Keshin, who was the top dog on the AT&T business by then. Everyone was annoyed, but no one did anything about it, at least not to my knowledge.

Oh, and our presentation wasn't good, even with that outside help. We didn't get the business.

My second run-in with Peter dropped an entire *bale* of hay on my back.

We had gotten into the finals for the Whirlpool Appliances business. This was a huge chance to add substantial revenue to the New York office, and everyone was tense about winning the account. I'd been on the job for about three months at this point.

I'd figured out by then that the only creative person Peter Kim trusted was Jonathan Cranin, a smart, creative guy whom Jim Heekin had hired a year before I came onboard. Jonathan was Jim and Peter's great hope at winning new business, since everyone else at McCann sucked, according to them. These three pals were always going out drinking together and smoking big, smelly cigars in their offices.

So I chose Jonathan Cranin as the group creative director assigned to work with me on Whirlpool. I felt that between the two of us, we could keep Peter Kim under control. But I was wrong.

As we prepared for our final presentation, Jonathan had about three campaigns that were quite good, and I felt comfortable with our progress. But Peter was worried. He took it upon himself to hire a freelance creative team to come up with more "out of the box" ideas. I found out about this at ten o'clock on the night before the pitch, when the freelance team and Peter came to my office to show me their work.

Our strategy was to help contemporize the Whirlpool brand, which was seen at the time as solid but old-fashioned, and to impress people with the innovative thinking that was behind

Whirlpool's new line of appliances. The freelance team—who were actually two very nice and talented people—had an idea that Peter was ecstatic about. Their campaign revolved around young couples that were setting up their first homes. Each spot showed a little slice of their lives and how they interacted with their new Whirlpool appliances. I nodded, even though it sounded dreadfully boring.

"What keeps this from being a real snore," they said, "is that all these people are topless."

They paused to get my reaction. I tried not to show any expression, but when they wouldn't continue without a comment from me, I gave them one.

"Okay, I give up," I said. "And why are they topless?"

"Because," they explained, "that's *real* and *honest,* and it's how young people who are just starting out in marriage really walk around."

"They probably also have oral sex on their kitchen table," I said. "Are we showing that in the commercials, too?"

It was strongly suggested that I was not able to understand this young target. They meant that I was too old to have anything in common with the twenty-year-olds who would buy these appliances.

"Do we ever *talk* about the appliances?" I asked.

"No," they said. "Not really."

"Not *really?*"

"But we see them *using* the appliances," Peter piped in. "It's all very *real.*"

"I know," I said. "It *sounds* real. And I know I'm being a hack and a philistine, but the meeting is *tomorrow* with a bunch of *Midwestern* product managers, and I believe they will have a problem with *nudity,* not to mention the fact that we *never see their appliances or talk about them.* At least, *not really.*"

"Well, we never actually see any breasts either," said the sweet-looking female copywriter. She was trying to be encouraging. "We'd shoot them from the back . . . of course."

"It's bold," Peter insisted. "People will notice it."

By this time it's 10:30, and I need some backup.

"Has Jonathan seen this?" I ask.

"Yes. He loves it."

Okay. At this point I know a little bit about Jonathan Cranin. If he truly liked this campaign, he would have been here to present it so that he would have gotten some credit for it. Instead, he was holed up in his office, two floors away. I call him and he comes to our meeting looking miserable.

"Do you think this is a good idea?" I ask him.

He shrugs and says in the mix of all the work, it could be interesting.

This means that he hates it.

At 10:45, I kill the freelancers' campaign. Peter says I can't kill it. I say it's dead.

Jim Heekin is called into the fight, and he arrives at my office at eleven o'clock. We still have an all-night rehearsal to do and I am worried as well and exhausted. Jim hears the campaign, and it appears to me that he has gone into shock, because he is literally speechless. Peter assumes that this means that Jim doesn't have a problem with the work. Frankly, I thought that, too, and with my celebrated negotiating skills gone the way of my patience, I break the Cardinal Rule of Male Confrontation, which is: Never oppose a high-ranking man in public. And I say to everyone:

"Let me make this easy on all of you. This work will be presented at the Whirlpool pitch tomorrow . . . *OVER MY FUCKING DEAD BODY!!!*"

Now, here's a good example of when to play the anger card. Polite conversation wasn't working, it was getting late, and there wasn't time to seduce or manipulate. In my fury I not only raised my voice, but I also failed to use one of the more politically correct words for the verb "to fuck" or the adjective "fucking." But I wanted them all to know how angry I was, and I needed to send a signal to *everyone* that the conversation was over.

We rehearsed all night and, as usual, we had too much content for the two hours that were allotted to us in the meeting. But we don't cut content when this happens, we just tell everyone to talk faster. (As if that would actually work. As if that has *ever* worked in the history of advertising.)

The next day, we made our pitch for the Whirlpool business. Peter and his partner used up an hour and fifteen minutes to present the strategy, instead of the twenty minutes allotted to them. We ran out of time and never presented the third creative campaign, the media recommendations, or the nontraditional media ideas that our account management team had worked so hard to create. And we didn't have time for the clients' all-important Q&A.

We didn't get that business either.

The straws on this camel's back are now accumulating.

Our next encounter was even more of a personal affront to me. I know that it's not wise to make a fight with the Big Boys personal, but just because we're women, doesn't mean we have more than two cheeks to turn. We are not doormats, okay? If the infringement is aimed directly at you, if a Big Boy is doing something specifically to hurt or discredit you, you can't take it lying down. I have always heard the phrase "Don't let the bastards *get* you down," but there will come a time when you will have to *take* one down, no matter how painful it will be.

Peter's third insult came when we were courting the Marriott Hotels and Resorts account. Peter and his team of strategic planners had dazzled these clients with their brilliant research and insights into the business traveler. Peter had really done a great job enthralling these clients, and his thinking blew away the marketing people at Marriott. They really trusted him. I later found out that his two "assistants"—Nat Puccio and Suresh Nair—had done the lion's share of the work.

The final presentation for the business was scheduled for a Tuesday, and five days before the pitch I still didn't have Peter's creative strategy, even though others had seen it and commented on it. Finally, three days before the pitch, late on Sunday night, Marjie Altschuler sneaked the strategy to me and begged me not to let Peter know. He was such a tyrant that even Marjie, who'd had a long history with him at JWT, didn't want to incur his wrath.

"Help me understand this, Marjie," I said. "The new-business director is *sneaking* the creative strategy to the executive creative director *three DAYS before the pitch*? Am I the only one who thinks this is *LUDICROUS????*"

When we pitched for the business the following Tuesday, the clients loved the strategy but hated the creative. I promised that if they gave us their business, I would hire a star and give them a great campaign. We got the business. I hired Joyce King Thomas, and she gave them a breakthrough campaign that was the envy of all the other hotels in Marriott's category. And we knew that for a fact. Their competitors told us.

After that, we at least had an impressive campaign to put on our show reel, but I made a crucial decision: I would not work with Peter Kim anymore. Now I needed a strategy to get him out of my life and out of "my" agency.

If you can't work things out with a superior and you don't want to be the one to leave, you can let the problem fester away until you rot, but that's not going to help your dilemma and it just uses up valuable time. Trust your instincts; you will probably be totally on point. As soon as you are relatively sure a situation is untenable, swing into action.

First be honest and *then* be shrewd. Be upfront about what is bothering you and see if that alone will correct the situation. It could happen, and hell might even freeze over. But don't walk into any meeting without a few cards up your sleeve. You will be a better negotiator if you have a fallback plan. This could be anything from the support of an equally high-ranking person within the firm or someone with a boatload of clout, or another job offer in the wings. But have *something*.

After the Marriott debacle, everyone realized that Peter and I couldn't exist at the same office. I requested a meeting with Peter and Jim Heekin, and led them to believe that I was going to resign. I was bluffing.

I knew that neither Jim nor Peter wanted this to happen, even though I'm sure that Peter would have been thrilled to see me disappear off the face of the earth. We all knew that John Dooner would be furious at *all* of us for not making this partnership work, and it would be a huge embarrassment for the agency to lose its first female creative director inside of a year. After all, they'd been trying to fill the position for two solid years, and when they hired me, all of my interviews in the press were about how I loved McCann and wanted to come back home. If I left after less than a year, it would be proof that *no* creative director could work at McCann, not even someone who loved the place as much as I did. I had them by the balls, and I knew it.

I also had two more advantages based on my relationship with John Dooner. I knew that John never took out his frustration on women, and he rarely got angry with creative people. Two points in my favor. He would heap most of the blame on Peter and Jim for failing to make our partnership work, especially since I had such a well-known reputation as a collaborator. I also knew what it was like when John got angry. Not a pretty sight.

And last, I totally understood John's "mosaic" philosophy. He put people with unique strengths in specific roles, and he needed everyone to work together to keep the mosaic in one piece. He had little patience for people who didn't do their part in his grand design, and even less patience for anyone who tried to undermine the people who were loyal to him. And I was definitely one of those people.

So, with no one backing down in this "showdown" meeting, the decision was made to try and work out our differences. Peter would stop commandeering the creative director role, we would work together on new business, and I would not only be allowed to see creative strategies *before* they went to the client, I would have to approve them.

This must have infuriated Peter.

A lesser woman might have capitulated and sympathized with his misery, perhaps giving his ego a graceful way out. Sometimes after women have a major victory, they start to feel sorry for their opponent. This is such a female thing. Honestly, what man would do that? I know so many women who weaken at the last moment, and instead of going in for the kill, they waver and get soft and sentimental. They think that the man who has been trying to shoot them down just needs a little love to be a better person. They want to believe that they can get an enemy on their side just by being nice to him. I know this because *I am just like these women,* so instead of continuing to butt horns with Peter, I pulled out a little S&M.

Although Peter had agreed to include my input in his strategies, it was like pulling teeth to get him to change anything he wrote. During one battle, I went up to his office late at night. His nose was buried in a book (he was a voracious reader), and I gently suggested a slight shift in what I assured him was already a brilliant strategy. If we could just make this little, tiny *refinement,* he would be a hero to the entire creative department. At the time, I felt like he was ignoring me, but the next day the strategy was revised and the change I had hoped for was there—and it was even better than I had suggested.

After that, I met with Peter alone when I wanted something

done, and some of the time he even listened to me. But he never acknowledged any of my suggestions. I didn't care. As Ronald Reagan is credited with saying, "There is no end to what you can accomplish if you don't care who gets the credit."

I guess I have Peter Kim to thank for making a man out of me. The last straw in my dealings with him happened during yet another new-business pitch toward the end of my first miserable year on the job. It was also the time I decided to throw in my lot with Jim Heekin.

We were working late, as usual, and the entire team of twenty-five people was gathered in Jim's conference room, waiting to lock and load on our plan of action. This was always a critical step in our new-business process—it was essential for everyone to sign off on a plan at an early stage. But Peter kept leaving the meeting to work with two of his planners, who were trying to get a strategic deck done for a different meeting the next day. Triage would have dictated that Peter concentrate on that meeting and allow Jim and me to take care of the new-business decisions, but Peter could never delegate anything to anyone. This is another common failure of many brilliant people: They believe that no one is better than they are at solving a problem.

We had spent hours sitting in the conference room, waiting for him to come back for a few minutes to "approve" how our plan was unfolding. Five minutes with us, then twenty minutes with his other team—it went back and forth for two hours. He kept us all waiting: Jim, all of the people on the team, and me.

And the last straw was falling, falling, falling toward the camel's back.

By nine o'clock that night, we still hadn't agreed on things like which creative campaign we would recommend and how we would flesh it out with our other disciplines. Finally, Jim realized that we had to make a decision; we were all too exhausted to spend the whole night waiting for Peter to come back to our meeting. So he took a stand, and together we made decisions about how to move forward and who would be responsible for each task. As we were wrapping up, Peter came back into the conference room expecting to resume the meeting from the point where he had left us. We informed him that we had already made all the decisions, and we wanted to know if he agreed with them.

"Who made these decisions?" Peter asked. He was visibly annoyed with all of us.

Falling, falling, falling.

There was a heavy pause in the room, and in the next three seconds, Jim Heekin jockeyed himself into position to become the unquestioned leader of the New York office. He looked Peter straight in the eye and said, "I did." All twenty-five pairs of eyes from the team moved in unison from Jim to Peter.

What Peter did next sealed his fate at the New York office and, eventually, at all of McCann. A simple sentence of seven words would set in motion a series of events that would ultimately change Peter's career and alter the course of McCann's history. I'm not exaggerating.

His seven words were:

"Well, Jimbo, then you're on your own."

You're on your own. How prophetic.

Then Peter stood up and stormed out of the conference room.

And it lands. The last straw. Not a huge one, but the camel's back is officially broken. Splat.

Everyone looked at Jim, who was mortified at the rudeness and disrespect his "friend" had showed him in front of his own employees. It wasn't the first time something like this had happened, but it most assuredly would be the last.

For me, it was the watershed moment I had been waiting for. I decided in those few seconds that Jim was worth saving, even though his alliance with Peter had made him unpopular at McCann. I decided to use whatever influence I had to get Peter out of our way. I didn't want him fired; I just wanted him out of the New York office and off all our business.

This was a very scary decision on my part, because in spite of all of his faults, Peter did have his genius moments. I knew that his absence would create a vacuum, and no one knew if his two wingmen (Nat Puccio and Suresh Nair) would take his place. And even if they did, would they be good enough? It was worth the risk, though, because our present course of action had "disaster" written all over it.

Whatever It Takes

I was determined to remove Peter Kim from the New York office, and I had two aces up my sleeve: Jim Heekin, who finally realized that Peter had to go, and Steve Davis, my old partner from JWT/Chicago. Steve had just been hired to be the president of Young & Rubicam's New York office. His first duty was to find a creative director, and the people at Y&R were hoping he could convince me to come back. They had been trying to hire me for the previous six months, but I kept telling them that it was too soon to leave McCann. Now I could see how a contract with Y&R could help me manipulate my situation with Peter.

We have a mantra at McCann and it is "whatever it takes." We use it mainly to prove to our clients that we are unrelenting in our desire to do the right things for them and their business. But it is really the personality of an alpha boys club. We will do whatever it takes to win. I embrace this philosophy.

I told Steve Davis that I would consider the move, but that I needed a good contract for my lawyers to look over. This is standard procedure. When I got the contract, I showed it to Jim

Heekin and said that I couldn't work with Peter anymore. One of us had to go, and I since I had another job offer, I was ready to leave. Jim agreed that someone had to go but said it wouldn't be me. He arranged for the two of us to meet with John Dooner and plead "our" case against Peter. We met for a clandestine dinner outside the city. During the trip there, Jim impressed upon me not to "pull punches" in explaining why I wanted Peter out of the New York office. He'd already had a discussion with John, and he wanted me to be a strong ally.

"I know how you like to sugarcoat things when you're doing unpleasant tasks," he said in the car. "*Don't do that now.* Dooner needs to hear exactly how you feel."

And so we met. I told the truth about how badly we were all working together, and that, after a year of being miserable and seeing everyone around me being miserable, I had to leave. I showed John my Y&R contract and told him that if he wanted me to stay, Peter would have to relinquish his New York responsibilities. Since Peter was a vice chairman of McCann Worldgroup, why couldn't he channel his efforts overseas and leave the strategic planning for the New York office to his two lieutenants, Nat Puccio and Suresh Nair? John agreed. It was too easy. I'm sure that Jim had already made this situation clear to him, and that John had already made up his mind. All I did was give him the final impetus for action.

Within a few days, it was announced that Peter would take on worldwide responsibilities, and Nat and Suresh would be codirectors of strategic planning for New York. I already had a personal chemistry with the two of them and believed that this was one of the things that would make us an unbeatable team. The day John announced that Peter would officially leave the New York office, everyone rejoiced. That was sad.

It was also hard to tell Steve Davis that since the situation had changed at McCann, I was honor-bound to remain as creative director. But there was very little honor left in me. I had lied to both Steve and John Dooner. I never had any intention of leaving McCann for Y&R. I was just manipulating everyone, even the people I cared about. It would take a full year for me to feel comfortable with what I'd done.

With Peter gone, much of the stress that had been suffocating the New York office disappeared, but the McCann people still didn't trust Jim Heekin. So my next mission was to help everyone in the office see the person that Jim really was, instead of the person that Peter Kim had shown them. It would take all of my powers of seduction and manipulation, but if we were ever going to be a winning force in the advertising business, McCann New York needed to be a family, and that family needed their Dad.

12

Woman on Top

What happens when you finally make it to the top of a boys club? Once you lead men, how much influence will you really have working side by side with them? Can you help them get more in touch with their "female" sides without losing all the strengths associated with their macho male sides? Can you make the office a better place to work?

Can a female boss create a female culture in a boys club?

Several years ago, there was a big spiritual revelation that an environment of "love" in the workplace promoted more efficiency than an atmosphere of fear. This was right around the time when people were discovering that "emotional intelligence" (a.k.a. common sense) might be more valuable in a leader than rocket-science brilliance that borders on arrogance.

I had been advocating a kinder, gentler workplace for years and getting a lot of flack from the men who heard me promoting it. But I realized that it's easier to want this than it is to achieve it, especially when you are in charge of men. And yet a female culture—

one that embraces compassion, nurturing, collaboration, and sensitivity—by its nature creates a more productive, pleasant place to work than an atmosphere of fear, danger, and macho competition. Maybe a combination of the two cultures is the perfect workplace; it would be exciting but still fun. Can you create this environment on your own? Probably not. I couldn't. I needed allies—men who drank my Kindness Kool-Aid and decided it tasted refreshing after all. In a way, it's even better to have a partnership with these men, because they become invested in the outcome.

At McCann, I spend a lot of time trying to help the men I work with get in touch with their "female" sides. This is a huge area of confusion for many of them. They can't wrap their heads around what I want from them, even though I am more than explicit. I am repetitive.

It's important for them to develop some female traits, just as I had to learn male skills from them. They should be more collaborative and less competitive with one another. The men try, but instead they become very competitive about who is more collaborative.

I want them to have more empathy for people they don't understand (like their female colleagues), but it's hard for them to take this seriously. They'll offer to get manicures with me as a bonding exercise, as long as I guarantee they won't have to wear nail polish. Matt Weiss, our intrepid genius at new business, even allowed us to wax his legs so he could "feel our pain." He only did *that* once. And one time Jim Heekin, watching me repair my lipstick in the lobby of a hotel, agreed to wear some of my lip gloss when I offered it to him. He didn't even know it was colorless when he agreed to wear it. (He liked it a little too much, if you ask me.)

Even with these gestures, I expect more from these men. They need to be sincerely sensitive to women, and to me in particular. I want great, big, giant steps, and when they fail to come through, I show my displeasure. One day I had the urge to murder them all because of my teeth.

On this particular day, I had a major meltdown in front of the most senior men in the office: Nat Puccio and Suresh Nair, the codirectors of strategic planning, Eric Keshin, the general manager of New York, and Richard O'Leary, the director of account management.

I am very fond of these four men, and as close to them as I could possibly be without being married to them. For instance, I know if they snore, because I've slept next to them on long plane rides. (None of them do. They say that I snore—and drool—but they don't have any film of me doing it, so there's no proof!)

I know what makes them frustrated and which foods give them gas. I can make them laugh when they would prefer to be angry, and I can make them angry when they least expect it. We've solved problems, won new business, and saved existing businesses together. We've held lots and lots of meetings together. I have practically *lived* with them, like a big, happy dysfunctional family.

On the day of my meltdown, we had just finished an important meeting with potential clients. When I returned from a trip to the ladies' room, I turned on the men loudly and furiously. They seemed surprised, because I usually veil my criticism in order to protect their sensitive male egos, but not on this day. No, on this day I was fed up with all of them, and I told them so.

"I'm sick and tired of being the only woman around here," I said. "Look at my teeth. Damn it. *Look* at them."

Nat and Suresh stared at me blankly. They are both extremely intelligent but totally guileless. This combination makes it very hard to get angry with them and then *stay* angry with them, but I gave it my best shot.

Eric ignored me and continued marking pages of the presentation we had just given. Because we have been partners since 1987, it's very easy for him to annoy me, and he has had a lot of practice doing it. I sort of love the guy, and that gives him permission to be even more annoying. Since he is like a brother to me, he knows I will always forgive him.

"What's *wrong* with your teeth?" Suresh asked. He is so *sweet*, I would truly kill to protect him. Usually. But not this day.

"Nothing," says Rich O'Leary without looking up.

Rich was one of the people Jim Heekin brought over from J. Walter Thompson. He is such a nice guy, I don't even know what he is doing with all of us.

"She has lovely teeth," he says.

"THERE IS LIPSTICK ALL OVER THEM!!!"

Honestly, I have just had an hour-long meeting with prospective clients where I charmed them, impressed them, *amused* them, and worked hard at sounding intelligent. And I smiled at them. I smiled *a lot*. I flashed all of my teeth *a lot*. For a whole *hour*! Teeth covered with bright red lipstick.

"Oh," says Nat, raising his eyebrows as if making a scientific revelation. "You *do* have red teeth."

"A sensitive, caring, OBSERVANT person would have noticed AND TOLD ME!!!"

"You have lipstick on your teeth," Eric says gruffly, without looking up.

"IN PRIVATE!!!" I yell. *"AND BEFORE THE FRIGGING MEETING!"*

I glare at them and they all glare back at me, for three, maybe four, seconds. Then they ask if I know when lunch is coming.

"Can't you get in touch with your female sides?" I plead. "Just once? Just a little bit?" I'd been asking them to do this for a couple of years now.

Then Nat says the best line of his life:

"If I had a female side, I'd be touching it all the time."

They crack up.

It takes all my self-control not to crack up with them. Instead, I continue to glare at them. There is silence for a few more seconds again and then they ask if we ordered the good sandwiches.

I leave.

These men are like teenage boys. I think they are listening to me. I think I have made an impression on them, but I won't be sure for ten or twelve years.

Seduction and manipulation are powerful tools, but is there a limit to what they can accomplish? Can we seduce and manipulate the men in our lives to be more considerate? Can we cajole or force them to be better people?

Most people will say that we can't unless it's already embedded in someone's nature, but I refuse to accept that. I think that if you are *benevolently* manipulative enough, you can get anyone to be less selfish, more collaborative, and marginally sensitive. If the stakes are high enough, if the people you are trying to change can take the credit for their improvement, if the rewards for sharing are greater than the pride of gloating, it could happen.

One of the greatest achievements under my watch was winning the MasterCard business with a campaign that has become not only famous around the world, but a textbook case for brilliant marketing. We won this business because the people in the New York office broke with tradition and embraced three female characteristics: collaboration, generosity of spirit, and empathy.

Although we had been winning new business at a respectable rate (Lucent Technologies,* Motorola, and a second division of Black & Decker, to name a few), in August 1997 we had the opportunity of a lifetime: MasterCard had decided to try and reverse

---

* Now called Alcatel-Lucent.

its poor performance by seeking a new advertising agency to help it compete against its archrival, Visa.

The MasterCard account was big (somewhere around $100 million in media spending), it was a blue-chip company, and because it was the underdog, it was a visible, endangered brand that would garner public support. Everyone in advertising cared about the outcome of the pitch and the survival of the brand. Jim Heekin gave the pitch "must-win" status, meaning that under no circumstances could we lose this competition. We had to beat five other agencies, and every single one of them was a powerful contender.

But we had our hands tied. The MasterCard organization ordered all six agencies to use the same positioning line: "The Future of Money." It had spent a billion dollars on this line over the years, using it around the world. "The Future of Money" was on every MasterCard advertisement in every country, and yet no one could remember it. So we decided to go back to basics: we talked to the consumer.

After a lot of primary research, we identified the MasterCard customers as people who were "good" credit card users. They only spent more than they earned for noble causes, as opposed to the Visa cardholder who always appeared to be on a ski vacation in the Alps. Now, let's say that both a Visa and a MasterCard user want to buy a fifty-inch flat-screen HDTV. Their *reasons* for wanting such an expensive item might differ greatly, all according to the way the brands are advertised. The Visa cardholder is positioned as a "high roller" and he makes the purchase because he feels that he *deserves* it. The MasterCard person is positioned as "the salt-of-the-earth" and he makes the purchase for the sake of the family, so that everyone can hang out together and watch TV on a screen the size of a small house. It's all about intent.

Our focus for the strategy was "The best way to pay for the things that matter." Jonathan Cranin was the group creative director assigned to the MasterCard pitch, and Joyce King Thomas had agreed to help out. She and Jonathan had the exact same ranking. They were both SVP, group creative directors, and they both reported to me. Joyce, however, was already very busy. I knew that she wouldn't work on the MasterCard pitch for Jonathan, but she would do it for me. For me she would even *collaborate* with Jonathan.

But even with Joyce and Jonathan, two of the very best thinkers in the creative department, we couldn't crack the MasterCard deadlock. Nothing we did appealed to the consumers who saw our work. And we tried *every*thing.

We had used up a lot of time and still didn't have the Big Idea. Then one day Jonathan stopped me in the hall. He said he'd been in the shower when an idea hit him. He reached into his pocket, pulled out a crumpled wad of paper, unfolded it, and read me this line:

There are some things money can't buy.
For everything else, there's MasterCard.

It felt as though someone had knocked the wind out of me. I asked him if he was going to give his line to Joyce. He hesitated. I knew that he didn't want to share it. No creative person gives a brilliant idea away, especially to someone who doesn't report to him. But in an uncharacteristic act of generosity, and with a little encouragement from Jim Heekin, he agreed.

Jonathan executed his line with wry, almost sarcastic humor, and his campaign was very funny. But it still didn't resonate with consumers. Then Joyce and her partner, Jeroen Bours, took the same line and came up with the "Priceless" campaign. The rest is history.

We were the last agency to present to the MasterCard clients, and they looked unhappy when they walked into our conference room. Many months later, we would see what the other five agencies had presented and understand why they were scared when they got to their last hope. They'd spent a lot of time and money on the pitch, and they hadn't seen one good idea yet. Everyone was into some futuristic place, having been forced there with "The Future of Money" as an end line. One agency even used nudity to make the point that MasterCard "has you covered." (I swear that's true. Maybe they hired that same freelance team that came up with the Whirlpool idea.) In that spot, a beautiful woman gets out of a cab, and her dress gets caught when the door slams. It's ripped off her body, leaving her naked as a jaybird as the cab pulls away. A MasterCard card appears strategically you-know-where because it "has you covered." It was no wonder that the MasterCard marketing team was in panic mode by the time they got to us.

When I introduced Jonathan, who would unveil his brilliant line, I said something very pompous to the MasterCard clients (Nick Utton and Larry Flanagan).

"Remember this moment clearly," I said. "A year from now, when this campaign makes marketing history . . . when you become some of the most famous marketers of the century . . . remember how you felt the very first moment you saw this line and the creative that follows." And I pointed to the line we had boarded and mounted on an easel, covered with a large piece of blue velvet cloth.

Jonathan's setup was brilliantly written and delivered:

"Although we can't help you get the pride and joy you feel when your six-year-old rides his two-wheeler for the first time . . . we can help you buy the two-wheeler." He ended his setup by going over to the easel and whipping off the blue velvet cloth, revealing his line as he spoke it:

> **"There are some things money can't buy.**
> **For everything else, there's MasterCard."**

Everyone across the table from us gasped and looked at me. I tried to smile without smirking.

When Joyce and Jeroen showed the first TV spot, called "Father and Son," these clients, who had been instructed by their consultants not to show one iota of emotion during any of the agency presentations, leaped out of their chairs whooping and laughing from relief. Even the consultants broke out in huge grins.

We presented nine commercials and twenty print ads that morning, and although I always love every new MasterCard spot, because they are always fresh and surprising, the "Father and Son" TV spot that Joyce and Jeroen created is still one of my favorites.

The spot opens with a father and son on their way to their seats at a baseball stadium. As they are moving along, we see the father buying things for his son. On the screen we see the list of items and their cost, and we hear actor Billy Crudup's young, warm, nurturing voice say:

Tickets, $28.
2 hot dogs, 2 popcorns, and 2 sodas, $18.
One autographed baseball, $45.
Real conversation with eleven-year-old son . . . priceless.

There are some things money can't buy. For everything else, there's MasterCard. Accepted everywhere, even baseball stadiums.

MasterCard. The Future of Money.

Both Jonathan and Joyce had two children and were devoted, loving parents, but only Joyce had the empathy to understand the universal longing people have to connect, and come up with a campaign to express that.

All of the original nine commercials were produced, and they ran during the first year of the campaign, in 1998. The only change we made in the original copy that Joyce wrote was that we never used the line "The Future of Money." The line ended up being dropped when everyone realized that they had a much more powerful idea on the table.

MasterCard's "Priceless" campaign did, indeed, make marketing history. It became the most successful global campaign in the world, running in 110 markets in fifty languages. Over the past ten years, we have produced over 450 TV spots and countless print ads and outdoor and digital ideas.

And it all might never have happened.

If McCann had still been operating in a chauvinistic, male environment, would those two disparate creative people, Jonathan and Joyce, have collaborated? Would they have been willing to share the spotlight? McCann did not have a history for that kind of teamwork. Too many men. Too much testosterone. No women in charge. But by the summer of 1997, five years after we lost Coca-Cola, everything came together, and we were a great creative agency once again.

Why Can't a Man Be More Like a Woman?

Can we help a man become a better woman deep down inside? If you pose this question to a macho, alpha male, he will not react kindly. But think about how you could entice him with a little seduction and manipulation—especially if you could answer that age-old question that all human beings ask: "What's in it for me?"

Once the men at McCann realized that tapping into their female sides was not going to kill them, they honestly tried to adopt some of the behavior I tried to foster. Rather than convert a throng, it's often helpful if you can convert just one big guy, one macho man that all of the other men revere and will follow no matter what. If a recognized alpha male can tap into his female side, then everyone can. Haul in a big one, and the rest will follow. My big catch was Jim Heekin.

The last great benefit that resulted from winning the Master-Card account was that it allowed Jim to temper his macho image and show the entire agency that he was man enough to act like a woman.

Jim wanted to personally thank all of the people who had worked for so many months to bring in the MasterCard business. I told him that there were about 180 people who had touched the pitch in one way or another, on the front lines and as backup, and so we decided to bring them all into our huge conference room so Jim could deliver his appreciation. They all filed in, almost all of them trying to stay as close to the door as possible so they could make a hasty retreat. They still didn't trust Jim. They still didn't know him very well.

Jim started to talk:

"I just want you all to know [*pause*]. I just wanted to tell you all how [*pause*]. How [*longer pause*]."

Then he elbowed me in the ribs, which was my signal to take over.

"What Jim is trying to tell you," I said, "is that he appreciates all of your hard work in winning this important new business. And," I added for good measure, "he wants you to know that he loves all of you. A lot."

At this point, the tears that had been pooling inside Jim's lower eyelids came spilling down his face.

Jim began weeping in front of 180 people.

I was *loving* this, so I added something else to further his embarrassment:

"I've been telling him to get in touch with his female side, but I guess he's gone overboard." I got a big laugh.

Within minutes after the meeting ended, it was all over the agency that our macho, manly, testosterone-laden leader had *CRIED* in front of 180 people in the conference room. Soon, all of the people in the agency who could draw (and we have hundreds of them) created caricatures of Jim sniffling, crying, or just bawling his eyes out. And the drawings appeared everywhere: in the halls, in all the conference rooms, in the bathrooms . . . everywhere. Jim loved all of them and never wanted any of them to be taken down.

It was a defining moment for Jim. In the space of five minutes, McCann Erickson's tough New York office became Jim's agency, and eventually the rest of McCann's global network followed suit. We went from mistrust to devotion, and that lasted through all of his promotions, ending with CEO of McCann Worldgroup, until he left McCann in 2003.

It's not very hard to win the affection and loyalty of men if you help them look good. You don't need to take credit for everything you do. The men don't even have to acknowledge your role, but if the place runs better because of it, as a leader, you win. And that's the only important thing.

Sometimes we forget this when we get to the top.

Five Classic Mistakes We Make When We Lead Boys

When we are the boss of a boys club, or even a club with enlightened men, we can't ever forget that first and foremost, they are still men. When boys allow a woman to lead them, there are a lot of strings attached. We are not one of them and they are wary of us— at least they will be for a while. It's almost as if they are just waiting for us to slip up so they can say, "Aha! We knew she would suck!"

Our instincts tell us this is true, and yet we ignore them once we reach our goals. When we forget this, we fail, because we make one or more of these classic mistakes:

We get drunk with power: We make it to the top and then seem to forget all of the negotiating skills that got us there. Our democratic, "female" patience is replaced with a more efficient "male" dictatorship. It seems far easier to just *tell* people what to do than it is to keep negotiating for peaceful collaboration. While it's true that men behave this way, they are forgiven for their behavior. Women are not. A man is not expected to be nurturing, so he is not punished when he fails to foster. It's different with us. We are expected to continue to nurture and collaborate when we get to the top, and when we fail at this, it's as if we have betrayed a trust. We lose our following. I have personally seen this happen. I have given women promotions because of their leadership skills only to watch them become different people once they are in charge. Loyalty becomes a mandate for them, and not something they continually try to earn.

The people who succeed are the ones who understand that to lead, one must have eager and willing followers. This is especially crucial for women, because we are still new at this leadership business. We can never take anything for granted, even when our power comes with a corner office.

The women who last the longest in top jobs are those who continue to hone their powers of manipulation for the good of the entire company. Don't expect people (men) to do something just because you said so. You're not their mother, and your skills of seduction and manipulation should never become obsolete.

We stop reading the room. I have seen this happen time and time again. It almost happened to me both times I came into a place as the boss. There is an arrogance that goes with being top dog. Suddenly, everyone is trying to read *you,* trying to second-guess *you,* and sucking up to *you.* This instant power gives you a false sense of security, and you drop your defenses. But just because you have a leadership role doesn't mean you are invincible. The people following you can (and will) nail you if you are not doing the job they expect you to do. Never stop reading the room to distinguish between the people who are watching your back to protect it and the ones who are using it for target practice. You don't want to be that green officer in the battlefield who gets shot in the back by one of his own men.

If you are brought in from the outside, your ability to understand the new company's culture is the first lesson of survival. If you run roughshod over the men you are supposed to be leading, they will always find a way to discredit you, sometimes with innuendo. It's the coward's weapon, because you never see it coming. If you are too tough and you don't make them rich enough fast enough, they will find a way to unseat you. You know this is true. You read about this every day in the press.

We become real bitches. I know you're thinking of the old double standard right now: When men are tough they are firm leaders, and when we are tough we are female dogs. I'm not talking about being tough or firm. I'm talking about being a real bitch. Sometimes this is a hidden characteristic that doesn't surface until a woman is in a position of power; regardless, these women are easy to spot. They treat their subordinates badly and keep them out of the loop. Instead of delegating responsibility, they micromanage and don't allow the people who work for them to do their jobs. (I know men who do this, too, and they are bastards.) Women who are bitches don't listen to anyone else, and they hoard information, because information is power. But the worst thing that these women do is treat the *women* who work for them even worse than they treat the men. I have seen this happen at places where I have worked, and I've heard complaints about this from women (and men) at other companies.

We can be strong and even adopt many of the male characteristics that we admire in men; we just have to make sure we don't forsake our female characteristics in the process. There are male attributes that are essential to learn on our way up the ladder, but these must be tempered when we finally take the reins. Being decisive is important, because top-down leadership is better than bottom-up (where the inmates run the asylum), but there is a gender difference here in terms of expectation. *This* is the double standard: As women, we are *expected* to behave a certain way, and when we don't we are criticized. For instance, a woman can be accused of being too bossy because she is *expected* to be collaborative, and when she is *decisive,* she is resented. All of these leadership qualities are badges of honor for a man. But for a female boss, they can lead to bitterness and even insubordination. It's okay to be decisive, courageous, and focused as long as we are also somewhat collaborative, nurturing, and empathetic. It's the cross we have to bear.

We take the reins and don't make rain. Being a CEO has become a very dangerous occupation. One would argue that at the top level, men and women are held to the same standard: Make money or get out. Steal money and go to jail. I saw a blog recently that stated, "How five [women] CEOs destroyed confidence in the U.S. economy." It didn't have a second list of five men who had screwed up. There is definitely a double standard, but no one argues with the almighty buck.

We forget that we have to be better than men. We live with this throughout our careers, and then when we get to the top, we forget it. As long as men and women are different, as long as we are battling one another for the top jobs, there will always be a double standard. Everything men and women do will be judged differently. This has always been true, and it will always be true. You can resent it, whine about it, and blog about it to your heart's content, but it will never change. We must always work smarter, think better, manage more humanely, and be more patient than our male counterparts. That is the price we pay for joining their club. Just remember that many of our female traits are ours alone. Men either can't be like us (they don't have a woman's intuition, for instance), or they don't *want* to be like us (remember why they don't have empathy—they don't *care* how other people feel). If we maintain our female superiority, we can govern a much happier place than any man can.

————

If you think the path to get to the top of the heap is hard, it's nothing compared to the difficulty in staying there. Wherever you are on this journey, there should be many touch points for you along the way, i.e., times for you to stop and assess if you are truly going in the right direction. How much will you really have to sacrifice to get where you want to go? We already know we can't have it all. Who said that we could? Some guy promoted that lie twenty years ago, just to make us feel insecure when we *couldn't* do it all. Life is full of compromises, and women will compromise more than men every step of the way.

A very dear friend of mine at another agency shared the creative director responsibilities with a man who didn't appear to work as hard as she did. (Eventually, everyone realized that he was just lazy and he was fired, but it took two years for that to happen.) In the first year of their joint leadership (which never works, by the way), she had worked on six new-business pitches, while he had done two. She and I both had reason to believe that although they were equal in every way, he made more money than she did. He probably negotiated better when he joined the company (right around the time she did), so he stayed ahead of her with each pay increase, even though their subsequent raises were probably equal. For a while this assumption (she never did find out if it was true) really got under her skin.

But she was wasting her energy. First of all, she didn't really know for a fact that he wasn't working as hard as she was. Maybe he *was* working harder, but she just didn't see it because he was toiling round the clock *at home*. Maybe he was good at some of the things she was not so good at. Maybe he resented her as much as she resented him. They were very different people with dramatically different styles. I tried to help her see the whole picture and also to feel less resentful. Besides, I told her, the more work she did, the better she would become, and the more clients she won, the more they would see her as the brilliant thinker that she really was. After a while she agreed. My only caution to her was not to take on so much of the work that she would wind up doing nothing well. Women often make this mistake. Although we can't have it all, we can still maintain a balance in our lives.

I reminded her of a speech that Jim Patterson once made, several years after he left the advertising business to become a best-selling author. Jim had always been a big supporter of women, and he understood the unique problems that women in business face, especially women on the creative side of advertising. In this speech, he talked about how to keep all of the important balls in the air and how to identify the ones it would be okay to drop.

"Think of life as a game, where you are juggling five balls," Jim said. "And you label them Work, Family, Health, Friends, and Integrity. You try to keep all of the balls in the air. One day you understand that Work is a rubber ball. You drop it and it bounces back. The other four balls are made of glass. Drop one of those and it will be irrevocably marked, scuffed, nicked, or maybe even shattered. When you truly understand this, you strive for balance in your life."

The biggest danger for women who are striving for success in business is that they mix up these balls.

Then you have to ask yourself, "Is it all worth it?" This is something each and every woman must ask and answer for herself. It has been totally worth it for me. I've loved working in boys clubs, and I love working with the boys themselves. During all of my years with them, I was never bored and I never dreaded going to work in the mornings—or over weekends, holidays, vacations, whatever. We were all in it together, and there were always a few little signs that I was making an impression on these men whom I worked with so intensely.

One night at McCann, when we were rehearsing for a new-business pitch that we would deliver the next day, Nat Puccio blurted out that he was in trouble with his wife of eighteen years. It was her fortieth birthday the following day and he still hadn't gotten her a significant present, but that wasn't why he was in trouble. He had called her right before our rehearsal to suggest that she enjoy her last hours as a thirtysomething.

"What did she say?" I asked him.

"She hung up on me," Nat said, sounding upset.

Everyone just looked at him, stifling laughter, because he looked so surprised. Then he glanced at me with a sheepish grin and said, "I guess my sensitivity training isn't kicking in." But at least he was aware of it.

The next day, we were all sitting in the conference room waiting for the meeting to start. We were all telling jokes and laughing—except for Nat. He had been staring at me intently for some reason; then he suddenly stood up, walked around the large table to my chair, leaned over with his mouth almost touching my ear, and whispered:

"You have lipstick on your teeth."

————

There's only one last bit of advice I want to offer. No matter where you are or want to be on the career ladder, there's a lot to be gained by working with men and learning as much as you can from them. The more you know, the easier it is to manage them if that is your goal. So hang in there, no matter how painful it is at times. One of these days, these men will come through for you, and all of your hard work will have been worth it. You will have made them better men. And any way you look at it, a good man is hard to make.

EPILOGUE:
HOW WE LOVE
A HAPPY ENDING

So did the untraditional tactics work? Did seduction and manipulation prove to be the one-two punch for a successful career? The only way I can gauge this is to measure the success of the company I so loved to lead.

From 1996 through 2000, McCann's New York office won an unprecedented $2.5 billion in new business; among those clients were MasterCard, Verizon Wireless, Gateway Computers, Kohl's, Motorola, Wendy's, and Avis Rent A Car. We are still winners at new business.

During the years that followed, John Dooner made the following decisions:

In 2004, Joyce King Thomas succeeded me as chief creative officer of McCann New York.

In 2005, Devika Bulchandani became the first female director of strategic planning of McCann New York.

In 2006, Mary Gerzema became the president of U.S. for Universal McCann.

In 2007, Lori Senecal became the first female general manager of McCann New York.

These are four women who are strong enough, smart enough, and clever enough to lead men *and* women in a quintessential boys club that is truly a meritocracy. I am proud to be in their company as chairman of McCann New York.

And one last thing:

In June 2007, on the occasion of his son Michael's bar mitzvah, Eric Keshin, that big, burly alpha male, stood on the bema in the synagogue next to his boy and wept like a girl.

AND I OWE IT ALL TO . . .

I found a press article of mine from March 2000, and the big headline was "Seducing the Boys Club." In the interview I mentioned that I was writing this book and hoped to have it done by the end of the year.

What a load of crap that was.

I never gave the book a second thought until four years later, when I conjured it up again while accepting the prestigious Matrix Award, which honors women in communication "who have made a difference." My difference was in advertising. In my short but witty speech I poked fun at the alpha males at McCann Erickson and mentioned the book again. There was a very accomplished literary manager in the audience, and she called me the next day. Her name is Fredrica Friedman.

"Are you really writing this book, *Seducing the Boys Club*?" Fredi asked. "It's a great title."

I assured her that I was, even though I wasn't.

"Are you as funny and charming a writer as you are a speaker?"

I assured her that I was, even though the only amusing things

I'd written in the last twenty-five years were only thirty seconds long.

"Let's talk."

So Fredi started it all. After I made two attempts at an outline she told me, gently, that I needed professional help and introduced me to "my left brain," a talented and determined freelance editor, Karen Kelly. Karen not only helped me organize this book, she told me when I was funny ("I just snorted coffee through my nose"), when I was boring ("What the *hell* are you talking about here?"), and when I was redundant ("In this paragraph you use the pronoun *I* twenty-seven times"). She is one of the most patient people I know, and she has read the countless drafts of this book as many times as I have.

After these two saintly women, I have to thank the best man I have ever known, my husband, Brian Goodall. Anything I say about him will be unbelievable, so let me summarize his role in my life by saying that without his unconditional love and unselfish support, I would never have had the energy to get where I am today. He is also one of the smartest men I know, with instincts almost as good as a woman's. That's the best compliment I can give any man.

Although everyone I met at Random House was warm and supportive, two editors truly impacted my book and my life: Susan Mercandetti and Julia Cheiffetz, who recognized that I was trying to write a business book that read like a novel and, when I veered from that model, gave me direction clearly and with a sense of humor ("Take off your business hat and put your novelist fedora back on"). I also like the fact that they are hot and smart.

I want to thank the women in my life who have loved and supported me: My sister, Dona De Sanctis, who has been there for me since the day I was born and always made me believe that everything I did was brilliant. (She is blinded by sisterly love.) My great friend Devika Bulchandani, whose insights have made me a better writer and whose absolute affection and loyalty have made me a better person.

I have to acknowledge the women at McCann who have enriched my life in more ways than I can articulate: Joyce King Thomas, my longtime friend and wingman; B. J. Kaplan, who has loved me in spite of myself; Sallie Mars and Dana Mansfield, who worry about me and support my idiotic needs; Susan Irwin, for her advice and help throughout this process; and my personal assistant of eighteen years, Mary Ellen Cloyd, who has always been loyal, insightful, patient, and smart enough not to take any guff from me. Ever.

Also, three women I never worked with: Bonnie Wilcox, who has been my unfailing friend and champion for more than thirty years; my cousin Marilyn Forbes, who was a great businesswoman and the only female role model I ever had; and Pimmi Seth, an elegant, insightful Indian woman, who came into my life late, but whose wisdom and kindness humble me.

I also want to thank the men I have worked with who have given me a wealth of material, mainly from their bad-boy behavior, but also from their moments of inspiration: Eric Keshin, John Dooner, Nat Puccio, Suresh Nair, Jim Heekin, and Frank Costantini. Also, my Bad Boys on 27: Dave Moore, Tim Kane, Dean Bastian, Gib Marquardt, Paul Behnen, Tom Jakab, and Hal Walters. And, of course, Tenney Fairchild, who helped me to be a better boss in his own way.

This would not be complete if I didn't mention our six horses, who calm our spirits and reduce our blood pressure, and our two Yorkshire Terriers, Pipi and Lulu, who make it impossible to wake up in a bad mood.

BLOGS, WEBSITES, AND OTHER MEANS OF VENTING

If you want to yell at me or complain about anyone else, I'm here for you. If you want to stay in contact, go to my website: www.seducingtheboysclub.com.

Or sound off on my blog.

ABOUT THE AUTHOR

NINA DISESA is chairman of McCann Erickson
New York, the flagship office of the largest adver-
tising network in the world. She lives in New
York with her husband, Brian Goodall, two gifted
Yorkies, and six beautiful horses.

ABOUT THE TYPE

The text of this book was set in Berkeley, designed by Tony Stan in the early 1980s. It was in-
spired by, and is a variation on, University of
California Old Style, created in the late 1930s
by Frederick Goudy for the exclusive use of the
University of California Press at Berkeley. The
present face, in fact, bears the influences of a
number of Goudy's fonts, including Kennerly,
Goudy Old Style, Deepdene, and Booklet Old-
style. Berkeley is notable for both its legibility and
its lightness.